Single Girl Gems

Khrystian Nichole Cunningham

Copyright © 2014 by Khrystian Nichole Cunningham
All rights reserved. No part of this book may be reproduced, stored, or transmitted in any form or by any means, electronic, or mechanical, recording, photocopying, any information retrieval system, or otherwise without written prior permission from the author and publisher, except for the inclusion of brief quotations in a review.

ISBN:0990715507
ISBN-13: 9780990715504
Library of Congress Control Number: [LCCN]
KNC Publishing, League City, TX 77573

This content in this book is designed for entertainment and motivational purposes only. The reader assumes all responsibility for the consequences of any actions taken based on the written words provided in this book. Readers are encouraged to seek professional help or advice. The information in this book is opinion based on the life, research, and experience of the author. The author or publisher assumes no liability for any commercial, emotional, financial, legal, physical, psychological, physiological, or spiritual damages incurred including, but not limited to, incidental or coincidental damages.

Dedication

This book is dedicated to the undying love of my parents. They are and will always be my biggest supporters!

Paw-paw, my angel from above; I told you I'd never forget you…and I never have. Ganny, I wish you could have lived to celebrate this book with me. You would have been doubled over with pride. Thank you both for loving me from beyond the clouds.

To all my single girls in the world…You are GEMS…always treat yourselves as such!

Acknowledgements

With God all things have been made possible. Thank you eternally for the strength and encouragement to keep going, believing in myself and providing a guiding light when my days seemed dark and cloudy.

To my brother, Nathan; you are brilliant and I love you for continually turning my dreams into visual concepts for the world to see as well. God has so much in store for you and I want the opportunity to witness.

To my daddy, Doctor Rev. Nathan C. Cunningham, I love you for feeding me with God's word, being the ultimate provider, and setting standards incomparable to match.

Mommy, you are my role model, ultimate stage mom, and eternal editor! I love you for all of your sacrifices and faith in me.

There are a multitude of wonderful people that contributed in countless ways to my experience in writing this book.

Gratitude to my family; the Cunningham's, Jackson's, Hall's and Phillips'- you are too innumerable to name! Thank you for your support and love on this journey called life.

Hanna K. Roach, my very first follower, fan, and most importantly, friend. You inspired me above all to just get it done and for that I owe you thanks!

I have to give extra special thanks to Tanchea Cole, Etienne Harris (no more writer's block), Brandy Hinds, fellow author SISTER K. Scott, as well as my cousin Brandi Preston for lighting fires under my ass each time I got lazy and just wasn't writing. Your encouragement was a blessing!

Chapters

Intro

1. Good Luck in Love
2. Dating Bad
3. Good Dates Await
4. Khrystianisms
5. The Single Girl Holiday
6. Random Rants
7. Those Awkward Moments
8. As the World Turns in Real Life
9. Gifts that Keep Giving
10. Scenes in Dating
11. New Relationship Rules
12. Open Letters to the Guys
13. Life Gems

Intro

I get it. I am not the typical single girl that adores spending hours in the mall shopping for the hottest trends and classiest pieces. I am not a girl's girl that enjoys spending countless hours having Waiting to Exhale parties, Sex in the City escapades, or privately reading 50 Shades of Gray and then participating in online book discussions of the steamiest scenes I can remember. That is not to say I don't enjoy any or all of that because let's face it; I am a twenty-first century girl and I stay on top of pop culture.

    To be a single girl in this day and age is to be encompassed with all of that and more. I happen to be an ordinary girl that started off writing an ordinary blog about, what I thought to be, my EXTRA-ordinary life. *Disclaimer* my blog and this book are about me; my life, thoughts, opinions, aspirations, family, friends, dating, excursions, and just about anything else I can think to share.

    When I first began writing the blog I did it because a coworker enjoyed asking about my dating scenes as she was a married woman that enjoyed living vicariously through me. Each morning, or during or conference period, she inquired the what, who, where, why, and how of my dating life. She became fixated on hooking me up with eligible bachelor friends of her attorney husband and I would have been all too happy to oblige except I felt she wasn't too keen on my type of guy.

I told her I wrote a blog and she jumped at the opportunity to get an inside look at the window to my single girl world. After a few entries I decided to take to social media and expand my enthusiasm to my friends, family, and other followers. I began getting numerous amounts of feedback through private messages and posts about the blog until various people encouraged me to pen my work in a book.

Alas! Here is my blog turned book. As you read you may encounter yourself or identify with things I have experienced and share or perhaps you won't admit it. Instead; you will laugh, smile, shake your head, or reminisce of the event as it transpired in your life. That's acceptable; I was that way once. Just keep turning pages; presumably you understand where I'm coming from. (wink)

Some of you may read this book and get enlightened. You may feel confounded. Perchance you may think I'm extreme, either way; it is all relevant. I will take, and, benefit from your feedback just as I do in real-time with my blog. Above all, I want you to experience some type of emotion just as I did while going through the experiences and documenting them. Writing has been a self purging process.

I've gotten out of my own way as it relates to goal-setting, success, higher education, and the proverbial dating scene. I have been a single girl all my life and at the age of, err...well over thirty I find comfort in the skin I'm in.

I do, however, want to caution you not to get offended by my testaments. The intent behind my words are sometimes misunderstood and misinterpreted. I'm unapologetically honest and if I smile in your face, it's genuine. Do not ask my opinion if you are not prepared for my response.

When I'm wrong, I say I'm wrong and with that; I stand strong in my convictions. I am exactly who God called me to be. All I can really say is that they that truly KNOW me…truly LOVE me❤ This is my life and it's nothing short of ***FANTABULOUS***!

~i love~

for those of you that frequent my blog you are; family, a loved one, an old friend, a classmate, more than likely someone that has touched my life in one way or another no matter how small, or at the very least a complete stranger. i answer to khrysti, khrys, khrystian nichole, ms. cunningham, and chocolate princess. you might hear me referred to as khryssy, khrys-ah, bookie, or lil' kathy. someone once called me silk. they call me k-digga. chocolatte. black barbie. onyx pearl. cheerio. and sho'nuff. at any given time you will hear me screech an ear splitting SKEEEEEEEEEE-WEE. i can almost guarantee at a party you will find me dropping it like it's hot and throwing back shots. that is me. if you don't know me for dancing, then you don't know me at all! i have dance fever, the music's in my soul.

i love GOD, His many blessings, the trials and tests He puts me through, His unmerited favor and His multitude of tender mercies. i love my life; even when i feel like there's a storm cloud over just my head.

i love ice cream. i love deaisha. i love to laugh. i love my family. i love to love and to be loved. i love my mama's gumbo. i love basketball and football. i **live** to make my family proud and to please God. i love every single one of the 69 i.v.i.e.s. of conspiracy. i love romance. i love now and laters. i love to smell marc jacobs, michael, cashmere mist, be delicious, no. 5 and creed. i love chocolate-caramel-pecan covered apples. i love to sing songs that i make up and probably only sound good to me. i love texas. i love sundays. i love to write poetry. i love to go and listen to it. i love for a man to sing to me. i love to read cosmo mag. i love music, especially r&b and old school. i love the holidays. i love a confident and cocky man, i love the book of ephesians. i love to travel. i love listening to live music. i love football season. i love massages. i love tight hugs. i love hurricanes from boudreaux's. i love going to concerts that are like parties. i love when my dreams come true. and most of all i love waking up to a new day knowing that God has my best interests at heart even when i fall short of His glory!

Creating my blog spot I, at first, didn't know where to begin. I knew it was going to be about my dating life, but I had no idea overtime I would combine politics, social issues and concerns, attitudes, and all other personal issues or apprehensions I had. My very first entry simply described all things and people I significantly loved. Of course the normal culprits are embedded, but those were my loves at that time.

From there I began to take note that us single girls are rare commodities and we should, not only act as such, but be treated as such. In that moment, I birthed **Single Girl GEMS.** Sometimes I use SG Gems, or SGG as most often seen on twitter, in reference to my "Single Girl GEMS". These gems are merely

Khrystian tid-bits of treasures used and passed along to other single women/girls/females/ladies...you get the point. Majority of the info is transcendent for everyone.

Let's face it; you are single until you get a ring on that finger, walk down the aisle in wedding bliss and say "I do." Regardless of the mind game your so-called man tells you. I want to stop now and make sure you understand that I am not a basher of healthy, well-balanced relationships in the least. With the right man they are great. However being single does have obvious perks (clears throat), so as a mature woman of dignity and character; I feel the need to share what, how and why I do what I do when I do it. They're "my little secrets". Or not.

My list shall begin here; though, you will see it frequently throughout this entire book and if you currently follow my blog you are in good company. You can agree or disagree, but this is how I've lived my singledom.

SGG 1. Take the time to get to know YOU first.
*Honestly; you can't be in a relationship with any one if you don't know what you stand for, believe in, trust, love, what makes you laugh or what upsets you.
SGG 2. Why buy the software, when you can download it for free.
*I'm sure you get the picture...if not keep reading.
SGG 3. Options.
*Remember at all times you have them.
SGG 4. Damaged people are dangerous.
*If someone has issues step back as they heal before you begin dating them. You don't want emotional baggage on your plate. Take it from me, in the long

run, it ain't worth it.
SGG 5. Believe in fairy tales.
*They do come true.
SGG 6. Don't settle.
*You always deserve more and you always deserve better.
SGG 7. Don't settle for anything less than butterflies.
*If you're not giddy and always anticipating being around them. Move on.
SGG 8. Anytime you have to compromise yourself, thoughts and ideas to fit in it may be a relationship you should avoid.
SGG 9. No man is worth your tears and when you find one that is; he'll never make you cry.
SGG 10. At all times look your best, even at your worst.
SGG 11. Stick with love. Hate is too great a burden to bear.
SGG 12. Don't settle for anything less than your best.
*Make sure he is on your level emotionally, spiritually and physically; otherwise it's a recipe for disaster.
SGG 13. Have more than one date a day.
*Keep your social calendar full. There is no reason not to.
SGG 14. Always keep a "Lawd have mercy" fund.
*It could be for those leopard print Gucci's or for that weeklong vacation you oh so deserve; but you must have one, some or a little put to the side for a rainy, cloudy or sunny day.

Single Girl Gem
-A precious and polished declaration for the highly prized woman that is fantabulous inside and out.

As I approached the countdown to the last few days in my twenties I started contemplating, as I'm sure we all do. Hilariously, when we're twelve we don't think; it's my last time to say, twelve. Likewise at nineteen, you could give a ding dang dong that you'll never see your teens again because you're so ready to be twenty-one and imagine to be grown. For some odd reason at twenty-nine, reality sets in. If you don't watch it, you could go into a major deep-down depression; otherwise known as a funk.

Folks start coming out the woodworks to remind you of how old you are and how much longer, counting down even the last few hours, of the last moments of your twenties you have left. They try and remind you of how things are about to majorly change. I am here to set the record straight. Life doesn't stop at thirty. It only just begins. It doesn't stop at thirty-nine either.

At forty an entire set of new-fangled life issues, wonderfully well and the dreadfully bad occur. It without doubt doesn't slow down at forty-nine. Fifty is the half-century mark, you better do it big. But heck, the way people approached me about turning thirty, I may as well have strangled myself right then and there, or went and walked the plank. It was foreshadowed that once you passed your twenties, it all goes downhill. I swear I heard loud, obnoxious scary movie music excerpted everywhere.

Perhaps that has been the case for some people. Nonetheless life is what you make it. You can sit and wallow over loved one's being lost, opportunities' being missed, doors slamming in your face, life just not treating you right or you can suck it up and realize life is…well, you know the big B-word I'm referring to.

You can't rely on other people to make things happen for you; you have to do it yourself. Don't rely on someone to make you happy, create happiness or allow vulnerability to permit you to make stupid, irrational decisions. Recognize life, as we know it, is not over until that fat ass lady sings.
XOXO,

Single Girl Gem #37
Be your OWN self-motivator!
Stop relying on constant validation from a damn man!
(It's sickening) Plus, you really don't want to give anybody that type of control.
Happy Loving Your SELF

Chapter 1

Good Luck in Love

Single Girl Gem #21
Don't!
Don't live with regrets.
Mend a broken heart, salvage relationships, build new bridges, pay off debts, and pray more often.

First things first; ask yourself am I a Keeper? What exactly is a Keeper? You hear people say it, often, in regards to a proper significant other. My definition is as follows: (n.) Someone wanting or needing to be kept or someone that is worthy of keeping around for as long as humanly possible.

Which brings about the next question: What makes or distinguishes a Keeper? Is it a person that gives you butterflies in your stomach? Does the person accept you and all of your flaws? Does a Keeper catch you by surprise or off-guard? Will a Keeper maintain the element of surprise? Do you recognize a Keeper when you first meet them? How does one become a Keeper?

Just as with beauty; being a Keeper is in the eye of the beholder. A Keeper keeps a smile on your face and your heart pattering. Sometimes you don't even know how the Keeper got there or who sent them, but you are grateful they're a part of your life!

The next step is, "I Do". Before the world-renowned, "The Secret" came out; it was always encouraged for a person to write down goals and plans, or create lists in order to elevate your life and self to a higher plateau. I've done it, you've done it…we've all done it. It's just a part of this crazy thing we call life.

Everyone wants the BEST and no one has a true secret to living and or obtaining this success other than hard work, prayer, determination, yada, yada, yah. You get my point. I highly suggest if you have never sat down and made yourself a list or prepared a vision board; you do it immediately and watch how far some motivation and determination gets you.

      Back a few years ago, true to my word, I did the same list for the do's in a relationship I want and the do's of a great boyfriend also known as future husband I want. Suffice to say; the contents of that list haven't manifested quite yet (sad face here...but, maybe NOT.)

      About two years ago; a new friend of mine said she had done something similar. She had no choice in the matter as she was required by a dating website she joined. With this particular site you have to tell them exactly and specifically what you were looking for in a mate. She said, the moment she took it seriously, honestly, and realistically (key word here is REALISTICALLY) she pressed the send button on her computer for the website to do its magic...and it did. She said within a month she had found the man, which she has now been married to for eight years, of her dreams and he was exactly what she wrote on her list.

      I say all of this to say; I believe in fairy tales. As grown as I am, and as much natural wisdom that I may have; I STILL, to this day, believe in fairy tales whole-heartedly. Call me a sucker for love and romance if you want. I'll take it and wear it as a badge of honor. You should too. (Wink) Don't let someone tell you what you are too "grown" to be doing. Don't allow people to place you in a box.

      Make yourself that list. It doesn't have to be because you're joining a dating website. Create a list of REALISTIC qualities you want in your mate. Don't limit yourself. Don't scrutinize the list either. If it is long…permit it long. If it is short...allow it to be short.

Make the list about you. Not what your mom or dad wants for you. Not what your best friend of thirty years thinks you are worth. Not what your co-worker told you to look for in a mate, but what YOU desire in a mate.

Be sure to include your deal breakers in there as well. They are fundamental and should help guide your list. I'll discuss the makings of deal breakers later in this chapter. Ultimately, once you make the list, keep your big mouth shut about it. It is not for you to share, especially with potential dates and mates. They shouldn't know what you're looking for. They should only know once you fall in love that they were exactly what you wanted. Doesn't that make for such a sweet happily ever after?

Being in a great space is the last crucial component of having good luck in love. HAPPINESS is a great space to be in. When you are happy; you smile more often, you feel more confident, you have more energy, and you give others happiness. These are all attributes that are inviting and allow you to not only love yourself, but others, as well. If you aren't at a place of happiness please, get you some. Find yours. Create it by any means necessary.

It has to be some form of curse to be stuck in the same spot chasing your tail, like a dog, around and around. The question will always remain as you sit idle or stand still; what do you do to change your current situation? Your individual answer is what makes you a conqueror, a mighty warrior in the world we live in, or a coward, a victim of what lies in front of you. Which do you choose? How do you choose?

Whether it's as simple as dating, receiving love, or as life altering as choosing a new career path, a life-long mate, buying a house, or purchasing a car these decisions have to be made and you are the only person that can make a sound decision for yourself. You only get one life on this side so make it count.

One Man's Trash is Another Man's TREASURE

I could not possibly tell you about happiness without discussing the opposite. It is important that through dating and life you don't get down in the dumps. So what you didn't get that one job you thought you were perfect for? So what you felt rejected time in and time out by others? So what, so what, so what to the countless other things you have running through your mind that signifies feelings of brokenness, disturbance, or stenches of funk you still have lingering around? Dust yourself off. Clean yourself up. Wash all the mundane nonsense from your mind and start again. Refer back to creating happiness by any means necessary.

Fact of the matter is: Everythang Ain't for Everybody! (Yes, it's bad grammar, but it's great philosophy!) Just because you didn't get the job you "thought" was perfect for you doesn't mean the "good and perfect" career is not coming your way. Just because that seemingly beautiful relationship ended, doesn't mean your "good and perfect" for-you relationship isn't around the corner. Just because you lost your mind, man, and money doesn't mean it's the end of the world. Ok...that's a little tragic...but you get the picture.

The point is life will sometimes deal you a card you're just not expecting...just don't ACCEPT it! Make it do what it do, Baby (in the famous words of Ray Charles) It takes time, heat, and pressure to create fossil fuels- an invaluable natural resource that we use up by the second. Ok. That's the fifth grade science teacher coming out of me, but it's logical and conducive to what I'm saying right now.

You are invaluable. You are a natural resource. God made you. Your value increases throughout your lifetime. The heat and pressure allows you to shine brighter than any diamond. You are a gem. Value yourself and your worth before allowing someone else to stamp a clearance tag on you.

If they don't want you it is their loss. You are of value. Imagine where Oprah Winfrey, Beyonce Knowles, Walt Disney, Albert Einstein, Steve Jobs, Vanessa Williams, Michael Jordan, and our very own forty-fourth President of the United States, President Obama, would be had they taken in to their spirit the fact that they were discounted as trash. Really?

Listen. This world owes you nothing. Not anything. So what? Keep it moving. One man's trash is another man's treasure and I'm simply telling you there is a message in the mess. Don't take for granted something covered, that you are too lazy to uncover, and miss your treasure.

Single Girl Gem #37 Worthy
You can be a whole lot of EVERYTHING and still not be enough. Don't allow someone else's issues to undermine your self-worth. You have value and those that truly love you see it even when you don't.

The Resurrection

Just when you feel a situation is dead and even sometimes buried, the resurrection happens. A renewing of your mind, an awakening of your heart, a refreshed attitude, an adamant desire for revival. The dead situation I'm speaking of could be ANYTHING that is dead-end: job, relationship, health, family, finances, you name it.

    The honest to goodness truth is that this unproductive or dead situation within your life can and will come often and without warning. Keep hanging on. The elder-folk used to say, "Just keep on living..." That phrase is all too often an omen of certainty.

    If you have yet to experience a dead situation just keep on living. But, on a more positive and uplifting note...If you are in a dead situation right now, feeling at your wit's end, broke, busted, and disgusted...just keep on living!

    Just as Christ was resurrected, although He miraculously did it in three days, there is hope in knowing our resurrection is indeed coming as well. We may not know the day or hour, but we know as long as there is breath in our bodies and we keep waking up to a new day; there will be NEW, different opportunities. What a difference a day makes?

That dead situation you are going through is just the resting period for your mind, body and soul. So rest in PEACE. Rest in comfort knowing that no matter how detrimental or tragic the situation may seem; God is still in control. Glorify Him through it all. R.I.P. that dead situation because sooner than later the RESURRECTION will occur. Just remember; the night is darkest just before the dawn.

In the words of Max Lucado on twitter: *"Next time you're disappointed, don't panic. Don't give up. Don't run away. Be patient and let God remind you He's still in control!"*
Happy Personal Resurrection day to YOU. Start today.
Inspired by this life I live and I'm loving my resurrection

Once that is done, the great thing is we have told the universe what we want in our ideal mate and he has found us because we have made a personal decision to change our mind about things we cannot control. We have set up a personal bank account of happiness. We've let go of past hurts and pains that may have occurred and we are not carrying baggage from other relationships into our way of thinking about potential spouses. Most importantly we've put ourselves first.

Our resurrection has happened and now we've found love or something kind of like it. Either way, you can't be afraid to love or to be loved. You just have to go with the flow and allow what may come. It could be happily ever after through confirmation or it could a grace period. Let's discuss the differences in the two:

Confirmation ❤

When you love someone, love is shown, not just said. For me; I always say, if you love someone, treat them the way you, yourself, want to be treated. I personally found biblical confirmation. "'And you shall love the Lord your God with all your heart, with all your soul, with all your mind, and with all your strength." This is the first commandment. The second is, "You shall love your neighbor as yourself. There is no other commandment greater than these." (Mark 12:30-31)

Maybe I already knew this scripture, or maybe I already lived by this scripture, but there is no greater feeling of your convictions than having confirmation. Love means seeing yourself in the person you love. Placing yourself in their shoes, and saying, "would I want this done, said, or given by me?" "Is this my expectation?" "How would I feel if I received this?"

All those type questions should rhetorically be considered when you deal in love. I love, love. At this point in my life there is nothing I want more than love. God's love, first, for sure and the rest shall be added. What about you?

Wasting Time OR Using Time Wisely

Both are a matter of perspective. I think wasting time would be equivalent to lack of growth that we discussed earlier. To not receive anything from the experience. To come from the moment unchanged, unfathomed, and ultimately none the wiser. However, if, when you remove yourself from the situation you are a bit wiser, you have been challenged and grown, you have a new outlook or better grasp then; the time was not wasted. It was a grace period.

Could it have been spared? Okay, that's another matter of perspective. You GROW through what you GO through. So, in essence, had you not gone through the time spent; you would not be the person you are or have the appreciation of life that you may.

Some Negative Nancy's (as we've all been guilty of being at one time or another) may argue that time isn't forever. Once you've lost it, you don't get it back; and that's absolutely true. But…we must speak in perspective. We have to concentrate on the positive and lend beams of light whenever capable and possible to others so that no one is ever left gasping for air, unable to breathe through mistakes, mishaps, moments, and milestones of our lives.

It's imperative for having and keeping good luck in love. Look for signs of those time wasters or time wisers. Those are considered grace periods in love. They have been known to happen at the same time. But…watch your perspective and make every moment count.

I boast a conclusion that you only need ONE. ONE. A single, solitary numero uno ONE time chance at any and everything. Stay with me here, because I am quite positive I will have some naysayers. However; I'm sticking with my conclusion. I'm sticking with the definitive ONE.

Think of the promise. You really, if you think about it, only need or, are required to need only ONE chance to play the winning lottery ticket and win millions. You only need ONE time to change your life and give it to God. You need but ONE time to fall in love to know a person is the ONE.

You need ONE great opportunity in life to catapult your career into something great. That ONE meeting is the chance you get to prove yourself. The ONE time you open your mouth for the first time is the ONE time everyone forms an opinion about you.

ONE is the amount of time you are born and that you die. ONE lifetime. It is also the only time you'll have your first and your last. It's the only ONE of its kind. The first and only beginning and ending. ONE. Tyrese Gibson sang a song about it that I love. My roommate from college and I would turn the song up full blast and play it on repeat. ONE. It matters what you do with it.

Seriously, what you do with that ONE and only chance or time is detrimental. It can't be taken lightly. You either maximize your moment, or you crumble. You get ONE; it's up to you to take control of it. Make it your ONE moment to shine as bright as a shining star. All you need is ONE. What have you or, are you going to do with your ONE? Make the ONE count.

Wants, Needs, Expectations

We have our guy. We have this great guy that's fun, exciting, he's into you, you're into him, and you've been soaking each other up like rays of sunshine as you lay on a beach. Have you ever been asked, straight-up, what it is you want, need, and expect from your significant other when you first began dating?

It could be a daunting question, seeing as how it's a three-part question, but the response could be even more daunting, right? Or not. Some of us know exactly what we want, others of us don't. Majority of us don't realize what we want until it's too late, or the opportunity is no longer present. Then there are others of us whom have known what we wanted, needed, and expected since we got out the womb.

I suggest you take a moment and consider or reconsider exactly what it is you want, need, and expect out of your relationships. Also, take it a step further and figure out what you want, need, and expect out of life. What is it you want, need, and expect for your day to day regiment in order to get to your goals?

Actually sit and create the list, your guidelines, put it on paper if you need to just like we did in our, I Do evaluation. Making lists provides focus which is the key to getting anything you want, right? Once you have focus, the vision is clear, and then the goal becomes attainable.

Same thing for the relationship: Once you have focus on your wants, needs, and expectations in your relationship; the vision and direction of your relationship is set and clear. There is no miscommunication or confusion on what you both see. The global positioning system, or GPS, is set and it's up to the both of you whether or not you're willing to spend the money on gas, upkeep, and maintenance.

Are you willing to go those miles? Are you going to take the same route, or does one desire to take short-cuts and dead-end roads? If you can travel the same road the goal is most certainly attainable and you are on your way to the destination.

Problem lies when you hear or set the wants, needs, and expectations without being genuine. Masking what you really want. Do not do that. Save yourself time, save heartache, and be authentic by meaning what you say, and saying what you mean. If it's meant to be, it will be and if not; it was your grace period.

Deal Breakers

Dating and being in a relationship, both are hard work. It takes patience, time, effort, compassion, effort, trust, respect, effort, and a special kind of person, among many other adjectives I'm not in the mood to write. Did I mention effort? Oh okay...I did. LOL

In deciding that you want to be with someone and love them for who they are; you also have to decide that you will love yourself FIRST and foremost, and understand your deal breakers. Deal breakers are the absolutes of any serious relationship you may have. Without being on one accord with your deal breakers, your relationship is in for a world of trouble, heartache, fights, arguments, trials and tribulations, I mean utterly doomed. Okay, I'm being dramatic but I'm serious as a heart attack.

Here they go...in my particular order:
1. Religious differences- Are you catholic and he's Jew? It matters come Christmas.
2. Moral differences- This could save you trips to jails, clinics, law offices, etcetera...the whole shebang.
3. Extreme Social differences- You don't want to feel

ostracized for who you are, do you?

4. Economic differences- It might not matter what they have or how much of it they have, but it definitely matters if they have GOALS and life-long dreams.

The Honeymoon's Over

A good friend of mine and I were discussing relationships and among the many faucets of the conversation the topic of longevity of said relationships. There is a stage in any relationship where you get so comfortable with your significant other and so emotionally stable with them that it's only natural that you begin to let go of any and all inhibitions.

This is the moment I refer to as "The Honeymoon's Over." It is when things are not quite the way they used to be when you first met. The old folks call it "courting". Putting your best foot forward all of a sudden is done. Usually, during this stage, the couple feels free to release all bodily functions (burps, pass gas, etcetera). Where excuse and pardon me were once said, it is replaced with laughs and giggles. Whispers of sweet nothings in your ear are swapped for loud shucks and jives.

Beauty, baby, sugar-pie-honey-bunch are exchanged for girl or a simple no-tag.
The endearing, romantic intentions you came up with to surprise and sweep your mate off their feet become few and far between. When before, money was no object, you find yourself crying budget. To take the place of spare no expense and order whatever you like, you say we don't need that or let's just share. All of a sudden there's no need to spend every moment together,

instead, you see each other too much. Someone needs space.

      I could go on and on about the infamous Honeymoon's Over stage. I could even go so far as to describing my own past relationships as in that stage, because let's face it, after eleven months with the same person; for a woman (or anyone for that matter) that's not use to long term relationships; it could get tedious and mundane.

      However, I can't feed into the negative energy of bashing a good thing. As easy as it would be for me to highlight negative aspects of my relationship, let's face it; you're lying if you say your relationship is perfect. There are imperfections in every imaginable relationship because they take work, although the work can be and should be worth it.

      I have to say, being still in the honeymoon stage feels amazing. Still receiving surprises that give smiles, not tiring of your moments together; actually, having the most fun when he's around. Romanticism is an everyday occurrence, and pet names are insatiable. A relationship that's A-okay and full of adventure is what everyone roots for. Can I promise you will remain in the same stage or constantly whistle a happy tune? Nope, but a girl sure can live in the moment.

Protect, Profess, Provide

I love these three P's of love and quintessentially-romance I discovered. They apply to both men and women and I'll explain how I've broken the words down to apply for both sexes.

PROTECT

• When you love someone you should protect their

feelings, more so, their heart from any hurt that you could potentially be responsible for. Be kind, slow to anger, and watch your tongue. When you're in love; you are vulnerable to your significant other whether you accept or understand it -and not in some goofy way- but in a way that only you, them and your heart should understand. Take care in how you treat each other. They love you and only want love from you. Give that to each other, it's the best gift.

PROFESS

- Open your mouth and tell a person how much you love them. No one in a relationship should have to guess your feelings for them. They don't deserve to live love in suspense. Tell them how much you want them, desire them, need them, enjoy them...just plain old love them. Take care not to make them feel disposable or expendable. And, uh, if you do in fact love them...don't be shy about it. Don't whisper or say it behind closed doors only. Love is not a secret, it's a gift from God and it is to be shared. Be open. Be honest.

PROVIDE

- Make provisions to be together, share, pray, and ultimately love each other. Create opportunities to spend time together and (some) time apart. Supply each other your basic needs. Learn about each other, spoil each other, and intrinsically love each other. Lastly, no one is perfect, so be forgiving. If we all knew what we were doing, we would all be sucking on lollipops, skipping through a field of daisies hand-in-hand with the one we loved, but that's just not reality. Pick-up the pieces from where you are and make preparations to live in love.

Peace, Lots of Luck in Love, and Hair Grease

Chapter 2
Dating Bad

Single Girl Gem 33
Watch who you date.
If they do "the fool" now, they'll do "the fool" later.

"I don't want to get married!" That is usually just a lame excuse to curb the pain, frustration, and/or utter disdain for a pathetic situation you have found yourself in, especially when your significant other, or anyone else you've been dating, has not proven to be "marriage material'. So, what do you do? You sike yourself out. You attempt to fool yourself and anyone else that will listen.

"I don't think marriage is for me!"

"I love my life now."

"I don't want to get married and change everything!"

Lies. All lies we tell to feel better about our situation so we don't suffer death by blow dryer for not having a perfect relationship or a steady stream of dates in our lives. Oh...but when you have that ONE...the line does change. Remember every ending is just the start of a new beginning. I've dated good and I've dated bad. I wouldn't be the true definition of a single girl if I hadn't gone out with a few buffoons in my hay day, so the following are true stories that I care to share in hopes to curb your enthusiasm for rushing into a relationship with someone you have a bad date with.

There are signs that signify danger, and by danger I mean, heartache. If this chapter can spare you in any way from trouble, I aim to help with that. There is hope out here for us single girls, but in the meantime; there's always gems to pass along.

Faux Pas

There are many times where you see someone and you automatically may think they look good; physically. If you think they look good physically, you could be blinded to think they will be good for you but...
Here are some of my particular personal instances when I've seen someone and THEN:
1. They open their mouth.

Whether their voice doesn't match what they look like because it's too high or too low. That's awkward, to say the least. The thing that is truly a turn-off is when they don't speak intelligible. Having an accent is one thing. A thing, that I must say, will turn me off if it's too heavy. I don't care if it's southern, northern, eastern or western, too much of anything can never be good.

However, the worst is speaking English that is so incomprehensible you actually do think it's another language. Can you say, "Yuck Mouth" which goes into the next tier of disgust? You see the nice looking person and then they open their mouths and it's yuck mouth literally.
- You can tell a ton of information about a person based on their hygiene. If you're over the age of ten bad breath, food smeared onto teeth, yellow teeth, all of that and then some says plenty about your character. Please for the love of all things Gucci, visit a dentist, brush your teeth and floss regularly. There's just something about fresh breath and pearly whites that can get you far. Ever heard of, "Have a coke and a smile"?

If they are vulgar, obscene or just too much for anyone on Earth to handle it's a major turn-off. You're embarrassed to speak to them in private, let alone bring them around people you know. You never know what will fly out of their mouth.

They have no conversation. The conversation always stops at, "Hi." with them. You're constantly in a tug-o-war of a very intense game of, "what you doing?" Okay, they're nice to look at, but you sit in a room only watching television, or watching other people talk, or the best dates you have ever had are at the movies, a play, church, or anywhere else you don't have to talk.

2. Your attitude precedes your overall physique.

There are some people that either don't realize they are nice-looking and therefore, their confidence is less than zero and you're constantly building them up. This is exhausting by the way. Then, there are those that have confidence from earth to Pluto, when frankly; they just look good, they have absolutely nothing else going for themselves. There's also the one with that overbearing confidence and they do have something going for themselves, however their attitude overshadows how they look and you could care less to be in their presence.

Filling Voids

Is it temporary? I compare it to tooth fillings or seat fillers. I may be wrong. Could quite possibly be wrong? It just seems as if, when a void is being filled; it is taking the place of something else. Like with a tooth filling: the original tooth/enamel is weathered away. It's no longer present. There's a hole...an empty hollowness, so it gets filled. It feels much better. That filling soon wears away as well, over time; after all, it was just a replacement or a fill-in to the void.

Let's take a look at the seat filler. They, again, are the replacements. They sit in the seat until the original returns. They fill the void of empty seats so that the stadium, or auditorium, "looks" full. It's a sham. Once the original returns, that seat filler either fills a new void or is dismissed because there's no real room for them. Ouch! I'm trying to help somebody.

For the person that's getting the void filled, of course, they're happy. They're good, in fact, they are great. But for the purely-innocent "fill" they may be happy for a time, but once they're worn, weathered, or simply not needed; they may feel used and abused. Better yet, on the short-end of the stick.

I may be wrong. Could quite possibly be wrong, but if I'm not...I just helped somebody see the light at the end of a dead-end tunnel. A tunnel they quite possibly were traveling alone. A tunnel, that once they see the light, they'll understand that tunnel was never designed for them in the first place. You are no filler. You are a gem!

The Proverbial Rebound

Also known as wait-listed, benchwarmers, basically; they just don't make the cut, and rather than dismiss them...you hang on to them, straddle them along for the ride and inevitably you will "like" them one day. They are saved like some get-out-of-jail-free card. The wildcard. You may not be guilty, but you know someone that is guilty of doing this...you may even be on the sidelines as we speak.

The rebound usually is the one that really likes you, too. They're impressed by you. They probably want nothing more than to be your main squeeze. They answer when you call, and if not, quickly return the call. They'll do anything in the world to spend just a little time with you, that's why it's all too easy to get a hold of them when you're lonely, bored or just downright broken-hearted from the relationship lull you're in.

However, to be quite honest; they can't do anything right. You critique them on everything they do; from the way the chew, to the way they attempt to hold your hand. Normally, you wouldn't have anything to complain about, but since it's the proverbial rebound, you can't stand anything they do or say.

You always find something wrong with them to discuss with your one friend that always asks about them. It's sad too, because they're probably perfect for you, but since your so-called heart is somewhere else, they just won't do. Poor proverbial rebound.

If only they could be the "lead" actor in your romance play, instead of the understudy. I think too many times we, and I use "we" loosely, but "we" get so caught up in Mr. and Mrs. Right; you know...the real thing, "the love of our lives"; that we get set and determined on a Mr. or Mrs. Right NOW. We think we have to have a warm body, or some one of the opposite sex to make us happy, when all the while we need to focus on building ourselves up. Establishing ourselves. Engaging in what makes us smile and happy.

Are you unsure if you are the proverbial rebound? Or if you've used someone as you're proverbial rebound? Here are some things to take note of: Now, this is not law. There is no sure fire way to tell if you are a proverbial rebound. The rules may vary from person to person, or may even fluctuate depending on your particular situation, but this is pretty much so, what it is:

Have you ever gotten a call from someone that sounds so distraught and needs to talk? You've dated, or er...slept together, been boyfriend/girlfriend at some point; let's just say spent some time together, but for whatever reason you're not together (at the moment) and they; either out of the blue, or sparsely call, text or email you? Well...I hate to tell you, but you are the rebound.

They need a voice, a warm body, a comfortable screw to get them through whatever it is they are feeling. Did you notice that soon after, you don't hear from them? Usually the reason you don't hear from them is because they've gotten their need fulfilled. They've gotten their fix. As my mama says, "they've gotten their rocks off!" So you sit and wonder why you can't have them to yourself or all the time or be exclusive and I'll tell you it's because you're the proverbial rebound.

Do you talk to the so-called "one" only every now and again; and sometimes it's few and far between? When you talk to them...it's like they're rushing to get all their feelings in. I call it making up for lost time (insert side-eye). They are either fishing to see if you've got someone, pressing the issue of why ya'll aren't together, or in an intense rush to see you or spend "quality" time with you? Do you find yourself totally into them, and you think the feelings are mutual; yet when it comes time to have "the talk" you find yourself bewildered and not able to read their feelings?

Don't get it twisted or get your feelings hurt...but I'm here to tell you-You are the proverbial rebound. Some of us may be in denial. Maybe they call a couple or even a few days after, but still (as much as you don't want to hear it) you are the rebound...or perhaps you're guilty of doing this yourself.

If it happens more often than not...sorry, but you have now turned into the proverbial rebound. Always there ready and willing. Because let's face it: You're really into them. You still think there's a fighting chance even though they've been in another serious relationship for over a year. Their married, but still calling you, so you believe that the one they're with fulltime must be doing something wrong. No sweetie! You are just the proverbial rebound.

Long story short; there is nothing nice or sweet about having a proverbial rebound or being the proverbial rebound. Just like the title, someone is BOUND to get hurt! So watch yourself here. Be smart in love and war...because everything is fair. You have to know how to distinguish between playing, getting played, reffing or just saying, to heck with any games...I'm more than a rebound! I am a reasonable adult and I don't play games with my heart, mind or body. Know your position in the game.

Friends With Ex's

This brings us to the ever-prevalent issue of maintaining a friendship with an ex. I've, personally, never ended on bad terms in the slightest with any of my ex's, whether it was an ex-friends, co-workers, or boyfriends. I personally just think EXtosterone (discussed in detail in a later chapter) should be extinguished.

When it comes to a particular boyfriend, in fact; we ended still being there for each other through some pretty tough and emotional times when at first, but we were both legitimately fresh out of our relationship with each other, and neither of us were seeing anyone new. We love each other, care for each other, and will always have a certain level of respect for each other. Any past relationship or not-so relationship I've had, ever ends with any ill-will or bitterness towards each other. Why should it?

With all of that being said: we are not about to be meeting for lunch or dinner, chatting it up on the phone, catching up, vacationing together, or self-imposing ourselves into each other's new relationships. If we're not together; we have moved on, very plain and simple. I personally don't feel the need to communicate daily or even weekly to keep in touch. Isn't that what social media is for?

Social media is un-evasive and you can keep up with each other that way. Through social media you can see the highs and lows of a person's life. You'll see the moments they care and are willing to share. If you want to reach out through, "liking" a photo or status, "re-tweeting", or "favoring", that's fine, also. All that other foolishness is unnecessary and inappropriate. That's about as friendly as it should get. Keeping it copacetic, otherwise, you stand a chance of carrying something over and sabotaging a potentially new relationship.

Questionable Motives

You never truly know what someone's motives are for the things they do or say. They are always questionable. To the person with motives I say, expose them. This year is all about advances and growth. Get beyond your petty motives. You find more with the light on than rummaging around in the dark shadows.

To the target, er...I mean, person whom the motive is intended, I say; live in love, eyes wide open, and grow beyond pettiness. Give them a show; give them something to talk about. Be yourself. They are watching it all anyway like a developing saga, or scenes in a skit.

Past is PAST

It never ceases to amaze me how quite often people choose to remain in the past. Some might argue past could be fifteen minutes ago and they would be accurate, however; I'm speaking of more or less like five plus years in the past.

If you have had a relationship with someone in middle school, high school, or college and you are forty-plus years old, why are you still feeling some kind of way about that past relationship? That person? The times you did or didn't share? I've even heard ludicrous instances where someone is still holding on to schoolyard feelings they had for someone in the second grade. Really? (Side-eye here) Get OVER it. In the words of one of my closest friends, "You're too old for that."

The most beguiling part of my amazement to those that remain in the past is the mere fact that: People will actually try and use those past occasions to deter you or sabotage any inkling they hear of a chance for you to enter into a new relationship, or just the mere thought of your future happiness.

There are instances, in relationships, where a significant other could have possibly had a legitimate full-fledge relationship with someone else. Could have, by all rights and definition been serious eight years PRIOR or, let's say, as short as six months PRIOR; and someone is still holding on to texts, letters, voicemails, and sweet totally-nothing shared in your ear. Really? Get over it. Move around. The relationship is over or, quite frankly; you would be together. I'm just saying!

It goes the same for past grudges. I've had to overcome this vice myself. Get OVER it. Put that energy to good use. Stop hanging on to things that are in the past, those things that do not adversely affect you in this moment are not of importance. Everyone else has moved on and you are still replaying a conversation from twelve years ago over and over again. Reliving highlights. Getting mad all over again. Feeling hurt all over again. Frustrated all over again. Get over it.

If this describes you, no one cares. You are stifling your very own growth. Get PAST it. Get out of your own way. If you have been the victim of someone bringing past information to bait and switch your feelings, please turn a deaf ear to it. Don't judge your current situation with situations from the past. They are not equal. I'm trying to help somebody.

Exclusivity Counts

Speaking of something sweet and thoughtful someone did for me, I made the mistake- and I say jokingly- of telling him I believed his gesture was, as always, sweet and thoughtful. He says, "Of course. I'm always that way. I've been telling you that."
I ended the conversation with one of those half smile emoticons.

I really wanted to say, "You're absolutely right. You always are sweet and thoughtful...with Sally, Jane, Felicia, Tameeka, Mymeeka, MoeMeeka, etcetera and that is precisely why I can't take anything you do or say seriously. This same sweet and thoughtful gesture has been passed around like a bean bag in several games of hot potato."

That would've been rude of me however, and begun an entire different conversation I'd prefer to leave buried deep inside the core of the Earth. I've learned you can't change people, their thoughts, perceptions, or actions. God can, but I can't and won't try to. No matter how much you'd or I'd or we'd like things to flow in a certain manner; it's just not up to us to orchestrate. Let things be. A polite "thank you" for someone's efforts is quite sufficient. Take it or leave it but keep it moving, don't waste too much think-time. Surrender that "thank you" that they're owed, smile graciously, and you've successfully done your part.

Accepting Compliments

It is absolutely acceptable to receive a compliment from a man and not think he is just trying to get under your dress or into your pants. Be gracious when receiving your compliment and always say thank you. Never down play the compliment. It's for you and you deserve it. He obviously means it or believe me he wouldn't have said it. Instead of, you have a beautiful smile, he could have easily said; tonight looks amazing.

However, a very common mistake some women make is allowing a man to give a derogatory or degrading statement. That is not a compliment, it's an insult. If he says anything insulting, derogatory or degrading excuse yourself and leave immediately. Trust me; he's not worth your time.

I feel the need to explain derogatory and degrading comments, because I know for a fact people, especially my ladies (who, let's face it...I write with you in mind) don't know or have a clear understanding of what they are. I'm not calling anyone stupid; I'm saying you could be unaware or naive...don't get offended, just stop reading. LOL

1. Yo' booty shole is right in them jeans.
2. You are so pretty, for a (insert whatever fits)
3. Oooh you thick! I like a woman that can eat.
4. I usually don't date your type.
5. You're so sexy, you can have whatever you like...as long as you return the favor (wink)

DOUBLE GROSS! Watch out here ladies. It's a jungle out here and these men are BEAST.

The Communication Challenge

I'm not going to say, "men are stupid", or "men have no understanding" or "men never get it", but the saying is, "Nobody can read your mind" which holds true today, tomorrow and forever more. Men, no matter how pompous they may seem are, in fact, not gods. As women, especially in a relationship, no matter if you're first dating, getting to know each other, engaged or married have to COMMUNICATE our needs, wants, desires, aspirations...I mean, the whole shebang.
Case in point:
You can NOT implement a ten-day plan (see the film Two Can Play That Game) without the man having a clue that he has done something wrong. There is no such thing as a silent treatment if the two of you rarely speak as it is. It's not effective. How would he know, you're not speaking to him; if you don't speak on a regular? What his mind says is that, "She must be seeing someone else because I haven't heard from her." or even "I wonder how she's doing." or "Dag! This play-off game is good; the Heat going is going to make it to the finals! I just know it!"

     The man doesn't automatically know to make the first move. We live in a day and age where women are bold, if not bolder than men, so men are accustomed to interested parties calling first, texting first, asking them on dates first, and any other firsts you could imagine. That's just the world we live in.

     Don't play games, especially with your heart. Communicate. Allow someone to hear where you're coming from. Whether they agree or disagree you've taken the first step towards healthy, active communication. You'll never resolve issues resting on an assumption that being silent will change a situation. All great changes occur with voices, speeches, public debates, marches, signs, and movements.

Challenge yourself to the Communication Movement. Address issues and concerns in a non-confrontational manner. Every issue doesn't have to be an attack or a negative encounter. Be creative and explore options to help another person, at the very least, empathize with your feelings and concerns.

A perfect key to great communication is listening and deciphering tone. Words mean everything as well, and when you have established paying attention to your date and what they are actually saying; you begin to notice significant differences in good dating versus bad dating. For instance, if someone says they "may" do something for you, or "may" come and see you, or "may" have you over…it seems as if what they "may" do is an inconvenience.

I could be overreacting, possibly reading too much into it, or just plain old doing the most. I just figure if you really wanted to do any of the above mentioned, or had any interest in any of it whatsoever; "may" wouldn't be the word used. Think about when you actually want to do something and you're actually excited to do it compared to when you're not really in the mood or not up to doing something. Which words do you use in reference to participating?

It all comes down to tone and action. If you find yourself on the lower fraction of someone's to-do list then occupy yourself with someone else, or something else. I have plenty of solutions which I will identify in a later chapter. Try and not be a "may" date and most definitely don't allow them to dictate your plans for any given evening with ambiguous answers or responses.

Whoever said that anyone has the right to call someone at the last minute because their previous plan fell through, no doubt, and they attempt to disrupt your plans assuming you have nothing better to do? I don't think so. Don't allow it. That's classic bad dating. A foolish person might consider the invitation flattering, but it's actually inconsiderate on the part of said person, to request your company on a "may" or at the last minute.

I'm sure they knew of their plans prior to the day of. Ladies, and gents too, the overall continuing lesson for the day is: Don't be someone's rebound or crutch. Now, be clear; if this is your nature, to at will and random be used as recreation for another person's pleasure; by all means, Do you.

However, for the more mature of us, don't settle for that. A person will do only what you allow, contrary to popular belief. Be better than that and expect more. You may not even be remotely interested, but especially if you are, make them earn your time. It's not something they can borrow any time they feel like it with no regard to your feelings. Say to them, "No. Better luck next time. Give me more notice."

They'll call back, but next time they'll factor in the fact that, yes, you have a life too. A good life at that, and if they want to be part; they'll respect that you're not sitting around waiting on the phone to ring and they're on the other end of the line.

     Why accept someone's borrowed time? Who should accept someone's love that's given half-heartedly? When one person is spreading themselves to other people and not committed? When one person treats love like it's the equivalent to going to the electric chair? Like love means you're missing out on something or losing all of yourself being in love? Who would accept love that's not honest and true? Who accepts love that's only distributed in private like it's a secret that must be kept? Would u accept that?

     No one should accept that. No one deserves that. No one is some one that is worthy of good love and decent dates. Truth is: It's really not for you to accept because that is not love.

Run for the Hills

As we've been reading, we see that there are always signs given when things just aren't quite right when it comes to dating and relationships. We all know it. Most women, with even a smidgen of wisdom, can feel it; but it's up to us if we are confident, strong, and independent of loneliness enough to actually run for the hills when the opportunity presents itself.
Signs! Oy vey!

     I've seen and been privy to many signs throughout my dating experiences. Some might argue that my deduction to follow signs is why I'm single. Others would say I don't allow wiggle room for mistakes. A few may say I'm destined for a life of singledom and unless I remove the rigidness I will forever be single. Le sighs! So be it.

In due time, truth prevails and a person's real intentions and true feelings dictate a righteous relationship. Of course no relationship is void of troubles, stumbles, or trip ups and I certainly wouldn't place any stock into that notion but my goodness; some things...you shouldn't have to be a glutton for punishment to.

In hearing stories of my other friends' single adventures; I know it's not indicative of anyone personally; it is just the litter of the pick. Men! LOL Here is some examples when you should, like it or not, run for the hills because it just won't get any better. When a person is ready to settle down and be true to you: they will, plain and simple.

1. When a person never wants to take pictures and the excuse is, "I don't do pictures." ← Run for the hills!
* Why not? Either because they have a "single" or "unattached" lifestyle they need to maintain in order to get what they get, do what they do, or see who they see, OR they're ashamed to be with you. Neither is a good alternative to a simple picture. I have literally seen instances where they will take pictures alright, but they're so hidden in the background or behind you that you're left thinking, where's Waldo? The other time they will actually are present in pictures is if it's only them in a picture alone, or they're taking pictures with others, but not alone with you. You reflect on the night thinking..."Did I go alone? Who was I with?"

2. When a person was married or in a relationship and just like magic; Wahl La: they're not! ← Run for the hills!

*They are a lie and the truth is not in them, especially the married ones. You ask the simple question, "What happened?" and they say, "Long story! I'll tell you about it. We can go to _____ (insert dinner or anything here that they've been trying to get you to in the past) and I'll tell you the whole story."
Now; why is a story needing to be told? Just answer a simple question with an as equivalent simple answer. They can't do that so, you can't listen to their explanation.
3. You can't go to their house. ← Run for the hills!
*Huh? If you're dating someone why couldn't going to their house, if even for a minute to meet up before going to the next location, be an option. Something is Wrong. I'm not saying what...just know you need to run for the hills!
4. Talking about an ex with admiration or constantly comparing things you do, times you share, etcetera to that of the ex. Do I even need to say ← Run for the hills!
*No one is saying speak ill of an ex, never that. But why would a person feel it ever necessary to consistently bring up an ex in casual conversation. It's highly inappropriate and could only mean they are on the rebound, or not fully out of the relationship. It is just weird.
5. They like boys! Egad! ← Run for the hills!
*Really enough said but for those that still don't get it: if you know a person is unequivocally a homosexual and at one time you and said person have pined over the same fellow! Uh! With this, and any of the other four previously mentioned, don't just walk, RUN and don't look back! Take it from me

Insecurity Reeks

There is almost nothing worse than an insecure person. That is, of course, an insecure person that has been rejected. Insecurity has a funky stench that you can smell from miles away. There are those that have personal insecurities that cause them to settle for playing the position the coach assigned them. Either, they are too afraid to play hard, and give it all they've got in order to try-out for the position they really want, or they require attention that can only come from acceptance from others and if you don't feel accepted; you're not confident or comfortable.

Another case of insecurities could be you feeling as if your forehead is too big and doesn't fit your face, so you wear hats or my ladies keep bangs. There are more subtle insecurities that force ladies to wear caked up make-up on their already overly-blemished face, or cause guys to leave lines on their foreheads from the use of a Doo-rag or spend X amount of dollars to have the perfect lay-down, brushed hair.

A more obvious insecurity is pretending to be someone you're not, misleading others through your actions and comments. My personal favorite is being a walking billboard for yourself and anything you've even slightly accomplished. There's no harm in being proud of your accomplishments but when a person asks your name and you conclude with your resume and an important list of supporting actors in the story of your life...you're doing too much

The most common insecurities are those expressed outwardly by means of weaves, acrylics, false bank statements, over-priced accessories and luxuries. But through all of those examples; I must say the funkiest insecurities are those of a rejected person. Be it male or female.

An insecure person that gets rejected from a job or position smells of sour milk-
the company, human resources, and anyone in the position or job they want sucks. At least that's what they feel. Instead of working on themselves and looking within themselves or even looking at the other person in the position as a place-marker to do better; they insult everything and anyone that's making it happen. Insecure. Do better.

That's the bottom line. Don't be salty when things don't work out. Use your setbacks as a setup for a comeback, plain and simple. An insecure person that gets rejected from another person, my goodness, that insecurity smells like four day old burning shit. It takes your breath away and causes your gag reflexes to lock up and chock you. Your eyes water and stomach churns.

A woman that gets rejected from, let's say, the man she wants, and Lord; don't let him be interested in someone else and is actually foolish enough to admit that to her, she then lashes out moreover her words become venomous. Not even against the man but against the woman he's interested in. "She's ugly, she's knock-kneed and she walks with a dip, I'm not hating but everybody says she needs to work on her thighs because they rub together..." ←Hating at its finest LOL
The woman is scorned, hurt and mad that the man doesn't want her so she's attempted to take the lady you're interested in down with her.
The man that gets rejected from the woman-

Does the same thing as a rejected woman, or my personal favorite: they attack the rejecter. "You're a dumb-ass, you won't get no better than me..." I could go on but I suggest you should've hung up the phone or walked away a long time ago. Bottom line: Insecurity reeks! Know that and run for the hills when you get an inclination of anyone else's insecurities.

Grasshoppers

Quick insect lesson:
The grasshopper is an insect of the suborder Caelifera. A species that changes color and behavior at high population densities and are also called locusts. Destructive to plants and characteristically has long, powerful hind legs adapted for jumping.

> *Khrystian Tid-Bit:*
> *It's also a cocktail consisting of crème de menthe, crème de cacao, and cream.*

Grasshoppers are also characterized, by muah, as those individuals that hop from one thing to another as if they have no rhyme or reason...no justification...nor (in some instances) any moral fibers. They hop from job to job, relationship to relationship, city to city or state to state, and, grossly, bed to bed. These said individuals are "finding" themselves. They constantly look for and are trying to discover what fits.

Change is a good thing. We're not talking about change here. In this case; we're talking about those that run around like chickens with their head cut off hopping from one thing (person) to another. The said individuals lack loyalty.

Loyalty is that little thing that's coupled with allegiance and devotion. Pick a lane and stay there. Be open to change, but never lack loyalty. It'll take you far. Others can recognize it within you and will in turn be loyal, allegiant, and devoted to you and what you stand for. They'll have your back and have strong desires to uplift you whenever possible.

7 Habits of a Highly In-Effective CHEATER!

This list is not partial to men or to women. It goes either way, for both genders. It's simply a list I put together based on factual experiences, stories, tales and true life antics I've seen, heard and just down-right want to share:

7. They disappear for unexplainable time periods.
6. They can't or won't hold specific conversations with specific people in front of you.
5. They're defensive when you inquire about anything.
4. Habits change.
3. They get "new" found friends.
2. You find yourself in arguments and debates with them that have absolutely NO value.
1. YOU ALREADY KNOW

See below for explanations

Number 7-Being sleep or losing your phones are the two most prized and overused excuses for the unexplainable time periods. You might also be familiar with the infamous..."I was working late."
Number 6-This one is tricky. Maybe they don't feel like talking or maybe it's rude to speak about certain things at specific times. Leave this particular one to

your discretion. There has to be a time when they can talk and you are around. And when they do talk and it's more so listening than talking...radar up please, that's a Highly Effective Habit of a CHEATER! Short answer; yes and no, mmhhmm, uh-hu...does not make a conversation.

Number 5- Really? You can't even inquire about the weather and the idiot wants to chop your head off as if you said something wrong. This habit also falls under Sir Isaac Newton's 3rd law of thermodynamic energy (for my fellow science buffs) they will try and transfer energy. Good or bad they will do it. That just also means, if they're doing wrong; they'll try and make you feel guilty. Switch-a-Roo and such and such! You won't even realize it until you've gained 20 pounds or your savings account is at zero.

Number 4- Duh! All of a sudden they love to go out and watch the game instead of stay in. They want to shop for new lingerie pieces! They have "new" restaurants to try, fragrances, meals and "tricks" up their sleeve they want to share with you or maybe not share and just tell you about it.

Number 3- Low and behold, there's this "new" friend they spend time with. They have "new" things to talk about and "new" work to get done. "New" interests and "new" information. There ain't no such thang as "NEW". Take it from me.

Number 2- Jokes, fun and games are a thing of the past; as you find yourself arguing, fussing and fighting over the smallest details. A discussion about which restaurant to go to turns into an all-out war and the next thing you know (surprise) you sitting at home eating a happy meal with no damn cheese, still hungry, but too

mad to get more food...and where are they?! OUT! All because you both were so "upset" with each other.
Number 1- Please! Let's stop pretending we don't already know when the relationship has gone downhill or when a roving eye has changed the game. You basically already know. You didn't need me to write up the 7 Highly Effective Habits of a CHEATER. It's already known by you. You felt it. Besides, the cheater is the only FOOL that truly believes they are getting away with something. It always comes back to bite them in the arse (ass, as my Uncle Tony says)

While we're on the subject of cheaters in dating I want to address the cheater and little more thoroughly during this chapter of bad dating. Most of our not-so good situations in dating and exclusivity will probably stem from the cheater so it's important we understand the different, but not limited, characteristics of them.

How Many Ways to Cheat

...let me count the ways!
Cheating, unfaithfulness and disloyalty, as you are aware, are all common intercessors of failed relationships. Not just monogamous relationships, but; business partnerships, friendships, etcetera.
I've come up with reasons people cheat, are unfaithful or disloyal!
1. Fear- most people hate to lose, hate to seemingly be the underdog, and they don't want to be one-upped. They must do whatever necessary to stay on top and "win". At least that's what they think and this unfortunately includes cheating. They cheat to get ahead or stay ahead, so they think. Have you ever

played a game of cards or dominoes, or even entered a contest with a cheater? What do you think they're cheating for?

2. Needy- the constant need for validation or stroking. If they don't constantly feel validated by you they need to feel it somewhere, like an addiction, and the first person showing them attention or validating the fact that they matched their shirt and pants for the day gets them all for themselves. The "yes friend" is loyal right? It is the one friend that goes along with all of the narcissistic schemes and plans? The colleague that loves all of the ideas no matter how much they'll cost the company or how far off the mark they are? Try and be careful of the fans. They'll lead cheaters in the deep waters and then watch them drown. But the cheater loves them, right?

3. Easy to Please- you have to be right? I mean, when something is exclusive that means not just anyone can have it. It's a limited edition. A worthy and true treasure that is only reserved to VIP's is someone that is exclusive. Clearly, cheaters are easy to please and ANYBODY can have you and get them off. They can easily be made to "feel" good! They get showed a good time. But as Oprah said; it's easy, fun, and great to have all those people riding in the limo with you, but where are they when you need a ride or catching the bus? (Don't worry...I'll wait!)

4. Greedy- they can't eat just one, they must eat the entire bag of potato chips. When they're done...yea; they feel like crap. Want to make up for it and beat themselves up but yet, like clockwork, the moment another opportunity arises (bag of chips) they're pouncing all over it!

The moral of the four; to the cheater: If you're scared...go to church! Get secure in your own skin; you don't need anyone to validate you. Take a look around you. The people you can really, truly count and depend on...these aren't the folks you should cheat! The deserve faithfulness and loyalty. Give it.

Above all that's been written in this chapter and above all you may or may not have experienced, there's hope. The fairy tale is still there. The story is still being written. Change comes. Happy loving somebody that loves you back.

xoxo

Chapter 3

Good Dates Await

"Enjoy the little things, for one day you may look back and realize they were the big things." ~ Robert Brault

Reflect on Purpose*A Poem* Khrystianity

When u look in the mirror do you see what others see?
Can you see the beauty and the mystery?
Or do you see a void?
You stare in your eyes and it seems like white noise...
Take a closer look, don't be confused
Just because you feel betrayed and slightly misused
You have too much to offer
And so much more to conquer
So, look in the mirror and see what others see
Find your inner beauty and novice mystery
In your eyes lies a story that from your lips can only be told
Step outside your comfort zone and watch beauty unfold...

I can truly appreciate the person that doesn't have to capture every moment socially, but would rather live in the moment. The person that's actually living their life, instead of documenting it is a gem. The person that can recognize the worth of the person or people they're in a moment with instead of scrutinizing it…just saying.

Dating is fun. I can't give the bad, without celebrating the good. Before we can even get into the dating scene, no matter how often you've dated in the past, or how many different people you've dated, or how serious your dating was; there are stages and things we must get right about ourselves before we can begin and be Mrs. Right for anyone else.

This chapter will explore what exactly makes for a good date, what's your dating potential and give a little insight on where and how to snag a date. Whether you're shy or outgoing, there are ways to bait a date and a good date always awaits. I'm happy to share several ways with you here.

My major rule of thumb for long-term dating is simple: "Don't expect something from your mate that you're not used to giving yourself originally". Basically, ladies and gentlemen; stop expecting, asking, thinking, giving wish lists and barking demands. And most definitely stop allowing outsiders to tell you their should of, could of, would of's. Seriously! I talk about this often, I talk about it with almost every friend I have; at least the ones that ask.

If you don't already travel, or fine dine, or buy yourself nice things; how in the world do you expect them to provide these things? It's the age-old teaching- "Do unto others as you would have them do unto you." So many of us are looking for Mr. and Mrs. Perfect that we're not even preparing ourselves to be that which we desire. You can't desire the fairy tale or want a fairy tale, but aren't unwilling to put in any work.

I'm speaking specifically to my ladies now. Think of it. How many times have you said, "I want an intellectual mate?" "a God-fearing mate?" a mate with a sizeable income, enough to where; if I don't want to work, I don't have to work." What about good in bed? Have a good relationship with his family, particularly his mama? Even the smaller, less demanding pre-requisites-like, "I want him to be charming, funny, honest, generous, and love me for me."

These are ALL awesome qualities to want in a mate, don't ever think I'm saying they're not. However, what I am saying is to prepare you. Be reasonable. If you don't have any money in your savings; living paycheck to paycheck, how dare you ask for some Knight in Shining Armor? Your idea of heavy reading, is reading Vogue monthly; yet, you want a man to hold a profound conversation with you. Think again. If you go to the local beauty shop, purse "party" or Harwin **just** to get the hottest knock-off Gucci bag; how could you possibly insinuate that this guy needs to get you the best designer bag or take you on a shopping spree?

You want a spiritual man, yet the only time you set foot in a church house is for a funeral and possibly a wedding, and that's if you're in it. You demand he be the one that "invented sex" yet you're a prude and wouldn't find out what it took to please a man if it cost you twenty-five cent. You want him to take you on excursions around the world, yet you've never gotten on a plane, train, or taken a taxi a day in your life. Is it absolutely possible for you to demand a guy have his stuff together, when you don't?

This is not to bash anyone. I'm simply stating the obvious rule of thumb. Expect nothing less than your personal best. Whatever it is you desire in a mate; make sure it's a mirror reflection of you. We are designed to be help-mates. Not these anchors holding anybody down. Don't expect anything from a man that wants to date you and potentially marry you except his respect. If he gives you that, he'll pay attention to the way you treat yourself. The things and people you like. The way your family and friends respond and treat you. He'll want to match and even do better than that.

If you treat yourself well. He'll know you're not easily impressed by him opening the car door or picking up a check. Shoot; if he asked you out, he's supposed to do those things. He'll understand that he can't buy you any old hallmark card because what you're used to is hand-made cards. If he truly likes you the way he's claimed the spectacular gestures are sure to come. If you constantly have to remind him the "type" of women you are, i.e. -"I'm much classier than that. I like _____. I don't do _____." You might not be living a life he can mirror! He most definitely won't try and do above and beyond what you're used to.

At the same time, you should do nice and thoughtful things as well. Become well-read and well-spoken. Invest. Be you. Be the best you. Be pleasurable to be around, interesting, and an overall great catch.

Keep in mind, at all times, our actions speak louder than anything we say.

It may be just me but there are some of us that can get into a relationship with someone and everyone else around can tell that you and your significant other are truly changed! And by changed; I mean *noticeably* in love, smitten, head over heels! Not because you're dumb in love either. Pretending each of you is something you're not. That's no good.

I speak of the kind of change that causes you not to drunk call an *ex*, or *"accidently"* dial a *blast from the past*. The kind where you don't begin an internet love affair with someone you meet off messenger. I'm talking about the kind of change that makes you not want to be caught up in any uncompromising positions whatsoever; so you'll be respectful, and thoughtful, and careful with all feelings involved; including the person you're not in a *"relationship"* with.

I speak of the type of love Outkast sang about in, *International Player's Anthem*! "...hate to see you cry, but I'd rather see her smile." There's no other explanation to me except... **Love**!
Call me the girl that leaves no room for error, or too frigid, or whatever; but I honestly feel like if you can't let all other acts of indiscretion go with all "*others*", how can you truly look at your mate and declare, "I love you."? It's ludicrous to me! Yeah, yeah people make mistakes and mishaps may even happen; but come on, do you really believe that?

Why are these phrases such as; sideline chick, honey dip, jump-offs, my number two, and so on and so forth used? Honestly, if you need a number two, you're number one is probably not doing their job and you need to let them go. If they were all of that to begin with, you wouldn't have room for anybody else, not numbers two, three or four.

Then there are those of us that can't find an honest and good person if we spoke to God and had him tailor-made. Ok, I'm exaggerating of course LOL, but seriously; it's very hard to come across those individuals that are secure enough within themselves to be mature, monogamous, and genuinely good-hearted toward a future with you. Or so it seems.

I know I'll step on some toes here, but maybe, just maybe it's us. Did I just say that? *Side-eye.* Especially if you keep attracting the same loose in the head types, generally speaking, maybe it's something you're giving off initially, or even, as time passes. I say today is a GREAT day to re-evaluate self.

Just take a step back, make another list if you need to. How many times have you seriously dated what seemed like the same person? What are some of the qualities you noticed that ALL the men you date share? It could be so much so that they seem to read from the same script. If, honestly, they are all different; well you have one up on everyone else and you're probably just not the best at picking a good mate, **or better yet**, keeping them. That being the case, you should work on that department.

But, if you're in the other group; it's time evaluate SELF, because now you know the problem isn't that those you're dating are habitual liars. It's that you are *"choosing"* to be with habitual liars SMH! ***Ready... Set... Evaluate!***

Within your preparation to be a great catch figure out some other things on your own. Are you a loner or just alone? I've always been considered a party girl. I don't know when or more importantly how this image or title was bestowed upon me; but over time it seems to be true. I know I've partied enough for at least fifteen co-eds in my short life-time.

Maybe it's because for a short time I owned and operated my own teen night club, or perhaps it's because I started my own promotions company, it could even be due largely to the fact that I worked for several local radio stations in their promotions department, and I partied for a living at one time. Possibly because I started hosting Monday night happy hours, or because during my birthday; I celebrate the entire month. Whatever the case may be...my mantra is, work hard, and play even harder.

Even with that life mantra I, however, sometimes just like to be left alone. Don't get me wrong, I love my close seclusion of friends, they're not going anywhere. Some people come and go; including, but not limited to, boyfriends, husbands, co-workers, classmates, but true-ride-or-die friends stick around through thick and thin.

Consequently, I love to catch a movie by myself, or go and have a quick drink and appetizer by myself. Occasionally I will call a partner in crime, to just shoot the shells with, but otherwise I'm good being by myself. This fetish began around 2008. I had been six months into a break-up with my boyfriend whom for the year and a half or so prior, I did everything with.
One day, I needed to get my oil changed, and they told me it would be about an hour and a half. Well

because I'm a teacher, and most of my friends aren't. I had no one to call in the middle of the day during the summer. An hour and a half was a long time to sit and be hungry in a car dealership, and the chips, salsa and margaritas from Pappasitos were calling my name next door.

I admit, at first, I was embarrassed to go inside the restaurant alone, then I tighten up, and didn't care. You won't always have someone at your beck and call, and what are you supposed to do? Go hungry!? Not me! So I went. I decided to sit at the bar. It was inconspicuous and pleasant, and there were a few other people alone there talking and watching TV. They welcomed me with open arms.

I ordered my drink and my appetizer and sat and looked at the television. Next thing I knew the bar tender and my neighbor next to me sparked up a conversation and included me. They weren't too talky, I could chime in or not, and I could talk on my phone or not, check social media, or email. I could even just concentrate on my drink and food. No one looked or stared in judgment and no one got too chatty with me. It was the perfect first date! Time flew. The next thing I knew it was the dealership calling to tell me my car was ready.

Now that you gotten all the preliminaries out of the way you're ready for meeting and greeting which for some can be a very tedious, intricate and down-right disappointing thing. Being a single woman has its hardships and challenges however, it also has its rewards and privileges. I've found that what you put into it is most definitely what you'll get out of it.

Many of us don't know where to begin. It may seem that everywhere you go, those around you are boo'ed up. That's vernacular for in a relationship. You begin to question where the single and, let's not forget, available men are. You even feel as though they don't exist anymore. I got to that point. Single men seem to have become extinct like the Tyrannosaurus Rex. You've heard about him, studied him, but never seen him.

I've been asked many times over; where are great places to meet guys? Truth is there is no absolute one hundred percent correct answer to that question. Sorry ladies, I know you were searching for a better answer than that but it's like asking me: where the perfect man is? He doesn't exist and neither does the perfect place to meet men.

However, there is a silver lining to that statement. There are, as always; many tried tested and true places that could be as lucky for you as they have been for me. Here's my list:
THE HOTSPOTS TO MEET MEN
#1. WHERE
Mutual Friends Parties
WHY →This includes, but is not limited to; dinners, receptions, and house parties. The friend of the both of you can give helpful and useful incite on the gentlemen caller you're interested in. More than likely, if it's a true friend; they won't set you up for failure. You'll already know if they're available light is on, you definitely don't have to guess.
HOW→ Ask the mutual friend to introduce the two of you. If they're a good friend, they've already got it in

the works. They've pumped you up, created a supply and demand and now all you have to do is deliver.

#2 Least Unexpected Places
WHY→ This includes grocery stores, gas stations, the mall and EVEN at a red light (tested, tried and true LOL) It's refreshingly surprising and you're guards are down. You're more than likely to come across as being yourself and natural. Nothing is rehearsed and prepped! This is the atmosphere, believe it or not, that you are seen as the woman handling herself independently. Think about it. You're alone (independent), running your errands (taking care of business) and you probably have a serious face on (I'm in charge of my life. I got it together.)
HOW→ Isn't it obvious? Just go about your daily business, living your life and concentrating on what's important....YOU. Once that's done...HE'LL come and when you least expect him.
The saying goes...Love finds you when you're not looking for it...or maybe I just made that up either way; it's true.

#3 Happy Hours
WHY→ It's a fun time of day. Everyone's there (hopefully) from work...so at least he has a JOB. It's an open forum of conversation, especially for those of us that are handicapped in the communications department. You can go in a group, with a friend, or alone. It won't matter, because everyone is there to unwind from the work day and relax. There is no customary reasoning behind going to a happy hour; so if you meet someone...so be it.

HOW→ Go after work. Sit at the bar. Order a drink. Someone will talk to you...even if it's just the bartender. The trick here is to look inviting. If you're uncomfortable in your own skin...everybody else knows it. It's like a wolf sniffing out the sheep so be calm, relax, drink and enjoy your evening. Don't get too tipsy. It'll cloud you're judgment and you must keep a look out for the fathom wedding ring remover. He lurks in the darkness, just waiting to tell the HOT lie that he's single. NOPE! NOT!

#4 Go Back to School
WHY→ There's nothing hotter than an educated mate. It speaks volumes. Enough said.
HOW→ Study groups are already essential. Why not study with a nice piece of eye-candy? Don't forget the carpool. Ask a question after class...of HIM. Share the class book. There's already a piece of property to share. On your breaks and in between classes, the two of you could grab a coke and a smile. Anyone up for a latte? No, not you Priscilla (fictious friend that attempts to tag along) I got this.

#5 Poetry Night
WHY→ You share a passion for the arts. There is always good dialogue in between acts. There's music as well to dance to with him and you have to be quiet when poets are up, so there's the prime time to get your sexy, quiet whisper voice on.
HOW→ Get up and go. They happen all over the city. Look in the paper, visit websites and find a location near you that hosts poetry nights, especially amateur poetry nights. The next poet that goes on stage just

may be seducing you through the mic. Call it inspiration...or NOT.

Those are enough for now. I'll give more ideas as you continue reading this chapter.

Dating 101

Dating can be extremely tricky and there is no sure fire way to insure you're doing it right. Every book, manual, seminar or training...nothing can prepare you accurately for life. All you can do is tread lightly, listen to those that have come before you (well, those that have experience), decipher what will/could work for you and follow your very own true and honest instincts. Here are some of my personal tested, tried and true tips.

When Meeting a Guy:
1. Don't Take His number
I never take a man's telephone number. No matter how pushy or fly he approaches me. If he hands me a business card or attempts to spit his number to me; I simply explain to him that I don't take men's numbers and if I'm interested I give him mine. Mind you. I could care less if he uses it, calls the same night or doesn't call until the next month; I've given him my number and I keep it moving.

2. Talk
When he calls you; don't shy away from the call. Make the date. Set it up. There is no rule that says you have to spend several days talking on the phone. If the two of you decide to see each other the very next day and you're available go! What are you waiting on? There's no reason to play hard to get, he understands you have

other men interested in you. Hell, he was! So it's not a surprise.

The Date

1. Chivalry is NOT dead

If he doesn't know how to open a door, hold the door, pull out your chair, walk on the outside closest to the road, take your coat, pick up the check, etcetera; leave his ass alone real quickly! Always make it your business to date a gentleman. He sometimes comes few and far between, but ladies; a man only does what you allow him to do. If he starts off not opening the door, it may be that he's just so accustomed to other "independent" women racing him to the door and holding it for him. So stand at the door. If he doesn't get the hints throughout the night; make that your first and last date! You could also option to let him know your expectations, because remember; I man can't read our minds.

2. Accept Compliments

It's absolutely acceptable to receive a compliment from a man and not think he's just trying to get under your dress or into your pants. Refer to chapter three. Be gracious when receiving your compliment and always say thank you. Never down play the compliment. It's for you and you deserve it. He obviously means it or believe me he wouldn't have said it. Instead of, you have a beautiful smile, he could have easily said; tonight looks amazing! However, a very common mistake some women make is allowing a man to give a derogatory or degrading compliment. That is not a compliment, it's an insult! Again refer to chapter three for specific examples. If he says anything insulting, derogatory or degrading excuse yourself and leave immediately! Trust me; he's not worth your time!

3. Dress to Impress

Always look your best. This is not for your date, this is for you. When we look great, we feel great. And when we feel great, we are more confident and comfortable. He wants you to look good and show you off, just as much as you want to have him as eye candy and show him off. It's a boost to anyone when their date is being noticed in a great way. Want the night to seemingly never end...look great and have a great conversation.

4. Don't Give Away the Recipe

Hold a conversation. Don't give an exclusive interview. Dating is no fun if you tell **everything** about you. Sure he has to know your nickname or the amount of siblings you have, he may even need to know some of your surface hobbies, like the arts. He doesn't need to know that the only time you go to see a play is at the hobby center; or that you only like musicals. If you get that intricate he has nothing to learn or try. This is what I call giving the recipe. You can tell him the dish, but let him be creative and want to spend the time to get to know and practice and taste all the ingredients it would take to make you say, M'm, M'm good! There are no surprises or spontaneous gestures otherwise. If he knows you like chocolate cake with strawberries on the side; he'll bring you chocolate cake with strawberries on the side! Let him figure some things out on his own. Allow him to get to know you. He may introduce you to new and exciting things you never thought of or would have imagined doing by allowing him to get to know you.

5. Take Your Behind Home

Sure it's the twenty-first century, but ladies: You've

demanded a gentleman from the time he approached you up to the date. Don't ruin a perfectly good evening by overstaying the welcome. Yes, you are definitely an adult, but just realize when you decide to stay the night after you've put in all the work preceding that moment; it's in vain! Give him something to think about (you) and miss (you) and want to see again (you)! How can he miss you if you never left? I'm just saying! Above all, have fun and happy *first* dating, K

"Learning" Each Other

Raise your hand if you're tired of the "getting to know each other" phase? At the start of every friendship, relationship, or any other "ship" there's the dreadful learning or getting to know each other phase. Yuck!

What's your favorite this or that? How many brothers and sisters you have? What are some things you like to do? Are your parents still together? Then there's the unspoken "learning each other's" How do you handle conflict? What makes you happy? What makes you sad or angry or indifferent? What are your limits with others?

It really is a never-ending saga. Maybe it's just me but I wish there was some type of file folder you could just read at your discretion and at your leisure to find out about others. Life would be so much easier especially dating in those early stages.

Dating Etiquette 101

It really doesn't matter if it's the first date or the hundredth date. It doesn't matter if it's a group date or just you and the honey. There's etiquette that goes with the territory of dating that I've come up with in order to help be a little more engaging and politically correct in your date life.

Etiquette rule number 1- Be punctual
*No one wants to be waiting idle for you. It's polite to be ready, or be on time for the pick up. It gives the impression that you don't care if you're late. It's also thoughtless. If you know you're running late call first, and soon.

Etiquette rule number 2- Put the cell phone away.
*You're on a date and it's extremely rude to all parties involved if you're phone is ringing or buzzing every 5 minutes, if you're answering the phone, leaving every second to answer the phone, texting, checking emails, or playing games on your phone instead of participating in your date. You just flat out suck. Of course the only reasonable exclusion would be emergencies; but trust me unless you're President Obama and there is a nuclear bomb about to destroy the world as we know it; I'm sure it can be handled in a more timely and polite manner.

Etiquette rule number 3- MEN: Be chivalrous, LADY: Let him.
*Have manners and allow a person to have manners and respect for you. There's nothing more attractive than seeing a lady and a gentleman together.

Etiquette rule number 4- Look into their eyes.
*There is nothing worse than someone that can't look

into your eyes when they speak. It's like you have something to hide or you're really not into the date. Don't act distracted or bored.

Etiquette rule number 5- This is my personal pet peeve. No pretention.

*You're not a used car sales man...You're not selling yourself to the date. Please, don't wear medals, accolades, or references on your chest. The great you will indeed shine through, especially if you're pure and real.

First Date FAQ's

Since a first date can be quite awkward and I don't know about you, but; I despise the mundane questions: Where'd you go to school? How many siblings do you have? What do you do? Blah, blah, blah...

Here are a few "frequently" asked questions that may alleviate uncomfortable silences and ignite blazing conversation! It could also give a greater insight into their personality without asking, "How would you describe your personality?" Feel free to add to my running list...

- What's the last book you've read?
- What's the most beautiful place you've ever seen?
- How do you measure success?
- How do you measure happiness?
- 3 worst qualities?
- 3 best qualities?
- What do you love to do in your spare time?
- Where's your next trip?
- If money was no object and you could go anywhere, where would it be?

You'd be surprised, as you're getting to know someone, just how "silly" they could be, or you yourself. That is not meant to be a derogatory statement at all. I understand that in logical dictionary terms the word, "silly" is deemed as having a lack of common sense, however; I'm using this word as a term of endearment seen only by close individuals to a person whereby you wouldn't normally see these characteristics.

This is not "them" in a professional setting. This is not "them" even in a large group of friends or associates. Sometimes, it's not even "them" with extended or close family.

This "silly" side is meant: at a certain point in a relationship with another person you begin to see a side of them that not everybody sees. It's exclusive. VIP's permitted only. It's not meant for everyone. It's an intimate moment when guards are down, masks are removed, the armor is off, and there are no airs. It's the unveiling....the REAL DEAL HOLYFIELD.

It's beautiful, if you're sentimental anyway, because it's an extremely vulnerable place when you are and can be your naked self. You become wide open for judgment, but again, not everyone sees it so it makes it that much more special. Letting go and being YOU, with your imperfect self is, nothing short of, fabulous. Sharing that with someone feels almost magical. Again, if you're the sentimental type.

If someone has shared their "silly" side with you, be honored. It's not planned. So many times we, just in human nature, are striving to be who we imagine ourselves being, rather than just being who we truly are without fictionalizing a character. Make sense? Fake it 'till you make it; meaning, when meeting and maintaining relationships nine times out of ten someone isn't always their authentic selves.

Why would you be?! They may not like the "real" you. It may be too much to take in. You may be offensive. They may not take you seriously. You might be rejected. So, in order to deny any rejection or even give-way to the clue we're not all we say at this moment, however, we're working on it; we put up facades. We "look" and "act" the part. Not fully understanding that in our vulnerable and most imperfect moments there's a beauty that's incomparable.

It's that "silly" moment when a person feels comfortable enough around you to be comfortable in their own skin; the moments you are a REAL person with quirky traits, habits, and idioms. Sharing your "silly" side, should indeed be limited editions. It's not for everybody. Remember exclusivity counts.

Historically, it has been men that feel the need to mask but with role reversal, women have been known to do it as well. No offense men. Men, historically, have always attempted to maintain their macho side and ego even when they really liked a woman. Now days, more often than not, however, women are beginning to feel the pressure to mask vulnerability as well.

Is that not you? Oh. You really don't get what I'm saying? Oh. You read back over this section and still don't get what I'm trying to say? Oh. You're your "naked" self at all times? Oh. What you see is what you get? Oh, okay. My bad then. Please, by all means, carry on. LOL xoxo❤

You'll know when it's real. You'll feel when you can show your "silly" side and when you can remove any and all masks you may have up. When you get to the point in your dating that one person, or you two have made it an official relationship you will know.

You don't want to keep it secret and neither do they. You want everyone to know and so do they. You'll say there name for no apparent reason and smile the entire time saying it. LOVE...when the bug hits all the other nonsense goes out the window. You actually want people to know you're in love. It's not just some secret only between the two people involved. As Stephanie Mills sang, even a little child could see. You feel good ALL over. I think if you deny it or act like it's not going on then you're not in love. Think about it and don't settle.

Ladies Beware

There is a trend in the dating culture that I must most definitely address. Allow a man to be a gentleman! Ladies, please stop degrading men and allow them men to:
- Approach you
- Compliment you
- Take you out
- Open your door
- Call you first
- Send you flowers or other small tokens of appreciation
- Tell the world about you
- Hold your hand

It's not "thirst". It's called **dating**! It's called taking an active interest in someone. In some places, it's even called basic common decency. (Clears throat) That place would be my mouth. Even within a relationship, if you've found a gentleman, you'll still be fortunate enough to date your significant other every chance you get.

Beware, however, to remain a lady. I can't say this enough. This is not just some after-thought I came up with on my own. Most men I speak to, whether a personal friend or not, when we're in discussion about relationships or when they're getting advice from me this is their number one complaint. Ladies, we're not appreciative of those gentlemen that approach us or come our way.

Be a gracious recipient. Use the wonderful phrases like, please and thank you. You'd be surprised at the amount of gentleman that aren't used to hearing those things. It's foreign to them, and sometimes uncomfortable if heard because they're obviously not used to dating ladies.
I'm dating someone that feels obligated to be a gentleman and thinks it strange that I would ever say, "Thank you for a perfect evening." While I understand the thought-process of feeling obligated, or I should say, thinking: I'm offering to take you out so, it'll be a good evening, and you don't have to thank me for that ...wait! Scratch that! I don't understand that thought-process! Never mind.

I'll continue to say please and thank you and he'll continue to be baffled at my politeness. We aim to change the "game" one "player" at a time. That was a slight joke. But seriously: allow men to be gentlemen and women, remain ladies! Always maintain that chivalry is not dead...well...at least it's not buried, so it can still be revived, right?

Stop calling men thirsty for wanting to show interest in you and attempting to spend time with you.

If no one was doing it; you'd call it a drought. That's exactly where you'll end up if you continue with this nonsense talk of thirst. These men are truly damned if they do, and damned if they don't with y'all LOL
~Khrystian Tid-bit~

Good dates await ladies, as long as we are kind, remain ladies, stay open to possibilities, and continue working to be the best version of ourselves. One thing we have to practice is not jumping at a man's whim when HE decides he wants to talk or spend time with us. Many times as single women we will "jump" at the opportunity to enjoy the company of a man or go on a "date".

      Some of us get lonely, others of us just enjoy the company of our male counter-parts, a few of us would rather have someone wine and dine us, many of us do it because we'll feel like some sort of leper if we don't go on the occasional "date", several of us prefer not to do things alone, and others of us just simply have nothing else to do!

      Well in all of my years of being single, dating, and being in relationships; I have decided to post a list of entertaining things to do and places to go when biding your time. Instead of waiting by the phone for the guy you just love to call and invite you somewhere. And instead of proverbially lying about faux plans and intentions you have for the evening; or even just not answering the phone as HE calls or responding to him, in the hopes he doesn't think you're some sort of "loser" for being home watching re-runs of The Game on a Friday night; here are a few ideas and benefits to partaking in them:

1. Movies

Take Advantage: Don't go during the PEAK "date times". Go in the early afternoon. Catch a matinee. No one is watching you. They're too busy watching the movie themselves.

Benefit: You catch up on all the movies you haven't seen. No one talks to you through the movie. You always find a good seat because matinees aren't usually packed. It's easy to catch a double or even triple feature. You don't have to worry about him complaining that you're dragging him to a "chick flick"

Time Not Thinking of Him: 90 minutes to 5 hours depending on the amount of movies you decide.

2. Shop

Take Advantage: Put on some comfortable kicks and you're free to maneuver through or peruse your favorite stores at your very own pace. Sales ladies are your bestfriends when it comes to making decisions. Purchase or just look it's up to you. Sip Starbucks or a smoothie. Get a make-over. Try on that bathing suit you're to shy too try on in front of anyone or that...shhhhhhhh, no less than two carat diamond ring.

Benefit: You don't have to worry about your best bud being dressed like you at the next event. No one rushes you to leave or demands that you stay. Get great ideas on make-up, outfits, and accessories. Most fragrance and make-up counters also love to give out samples! You'll always know what you want for a gift when asked.

Time Not Thinking of Him: 30 minutes to an endless time (there are always 24 hour Walmarts)

3. Book Store

Take Advantage: Sit and lounge reading your favorite magazine or book. Bask in the solitude of your own

thoughts, or just be lazy and get lost in someones else's world!
Benefit: Takes you away from the daily stresses of life. Catch up on some studying, get exposed to a new language, or learn some new information. Lots of times you'll find book clubs, poetry readings and writing seminars or classes that interest you. Expansion of vocabulary, current event topics, and OMG facts!
Time Not Thinking of Him: Approximately 3 to 5 solid hours (Endless if you make a purchase and go home)

4. Take a Class
Take Advantage: Yoga, dance, kick-boxing, cooking, art. The possibilities are endless! Sometimes you can find cheap classes at your local YMCA. For cheap dance lessons look me up: www.crowdpleasers.org (shameless plug)
Benefit: You now have a new fun exciting hobby that takes your time and energy; and you're learning something you ENJOY! You've expanded your communication skills and now have something exciting to share with someone. Many new hang-out buddies as well that share a common interest with you.
Time Not Thinking of Him: 30 minutes -1 hour

5. Workout
Take Advantage: That New Year's resolution sounds pretty great here. Gyms are a great place to get motivated and healthy; especially if you go right after work or mid-morning if you can. No one is worried that you're there alone they're shedding pounds and toning up just like you! They have fun classes offered at most gyms that will introduce you to others with the same goals and work-out plans as you.
Benefit: You'll feel great, look great and it'll become

habitual. The next time you go out; those favorite jeans will hug your curves just right. You'll be bootylicious!
Time Not Thinking of Him: 30 minutes. to 2 hours

6. Cook Dinner

Take Advantage: There are numerous online recipe sites that have some brilliant and fun recipes to try and re-create in the privacy and comfort of your own home. Watch a cooking show or any of the other food network television shows. While you're at the book store find a good cook book on sale. The last one I found on Creole cooking was $2.99 (NICE!)

Benefit: When the time comes to host dinner parties, wine and cheeses or a good old-fashioned get-togethers you'll have a plethora of ideas and to die for recipes that your friends will be begging you for. Brushing up and honing in on those cooking skills aren't a bad idea either. They say the way to a man's heart is through his stomach. You most definitely don't want to do trial and error on your proposed hunny or friends for that matter.
Time Not Thinking of Him: 20 minutes to 2 hours

7. Visit a relative or friend

Take Advantage: Whether it's down the street, around the corner or in another state. Time spent with loved ones and people that care about you is a great idea! Use all the new information you've been seeing at the movies or reading about in those books, or cooking on that stove and again practice those communication skills.

Benefit: Catch up. Nothing like the company of a loved one to remind you of the importance of just being you, it'll be like a mini vacation.
Time Not Thinking of Him: Endless

8. Update your page

Take Advantage: All those social media sites. Make it happen. Now is the perfect time to change the song, add a blog or note, go search for new friends, or re-connect with old friends.

Benefit: You won't have to wait by a phone or computer for him. You'll be so busy keeping up with everyone else. Infact, don't be surprised if your online light prompts him to no doubt call, text, email, chat, tweet, or direct message you. LOL and SMDH!

Time Not Thinking of Him: 10 minutes to hours (don't go past 3 hours though. Your head will start hurting and you'll get hungry or cotton mouth)

Happy Solo Dating!

The Meet Part Deux

Take note that meeting men is recommendations for where to MEET men, not FIND them. The key is to make yourself accessible, not hunt for any man. Know this above all else.

There are, as always; many tried, tested and true places that could be as lucky for you as they have been for me.

Keep in mind; there is no perfect place or ideal situation. Just go out and be approachable, savvy, smart, laugh, live and enjoy love coming to you. It's not complicated it just takes patience. As promised; here are some additional hot spots to meet:

#6 Weddings

WHY→ Love is already in the air. The water, champagne, the ambiance, it's already set up, so why not bask within it? You're dressed up and looking great, they are too. Enjoy the moment!

HOW→ Get there. Just because you don't officially

have a plus one doesn't mean you should decline. He could possibly be there. He could be the wedding singer or the groomsmen, or a fraternity brother, or a relative of the family member. You get the point. Mingle, dance, laugh, smile, and get introduced to unfamiliar, unattached faces.

#7 The Gym

WHY→ Everyone is into fitness. Everyone wants to be healthy. At least you know he takes pride in his appearance and health and he'll motivate you to do the same.

HOW→ Get off your lazy tush and go. Put on your little cute workout gear, pin your hair up, add a little mascara and lip gloss, but please, for the love of all things Chanel; do NOT go into that gym with a full face of makeup. Pop a squat, do some reps, even take a class. If he likes what he sees he'll come over. You two can turn into workout buddies and better yet; life-long mates.

#8 On Vacation

WHY→ If you love to travel, you found someone else that does too. There's no stress, no worries, and no real responsibilities. Get to know each other on a fun, friendly and flirty level first.

HOW→ You're looking and acting like a barrel of fun. That positive energy WILL attract a positive person. Share a drink in the lobby of the hotel, meet for breakfast or lunch. Again meet, not wake up to breakfast. Always remember you are a L.A.D.Y first. Hang out on the beach together, your group and his group meet at a party or club together that way no one feels committed. Afterwards; stay connected through exchanging numbers, email, or other social media.

#9 Workshops
WHY→ Any type of professional development broadens your horizons and elevates you to new levels. If you're stagnant professionally, you'll be stagnant in life and most definitely in dating.
HOW→ Sign-up. Network. You already have something in common, now all you have to do is build a personal relationship. And that's what all relationships are about anyway...building. Sit at the table with those attractive men, be open, discuss, don't get into anything too deep, but certainly don't be a wall flower.
#10 Gas Station
WHY→ You might find this one funny right, but EVERYONE needs gas, so everyone goes there. If you're filling up, you'll probably be there for awhile and that's just enough time to *spark* or not. If he offers to pump it for you and fill you up...he's a KEEPER! LOL just kidding...a little (wink)
HOW→ Duh! Get the gas...they will come.

No stress, just have fun and live life regularly. Go out, be approachable, savvy, smart, laugh, live and enjoy love coming to you. You have nothing to lose. If you continue just standing in the same spot, doing the same thing that would be insanity. Happy Meeting.

Lastly, as it relates to good dating, above all else once you have someone you enjoy, like, and want to spend your time with fall in friends. I use to wonder why the phrase, "fall in love" is used. I've come up with my own validated reasoning behind it. Falling in love is synonymous with when you "fall" into something or over something or "fall" down.

When you usually fall it's unexpected, exhilarating, jolting, scary, can be life-changing, etcetera and that's everything love is and more. Falling in love is great, but I feel people should "fall" in friends first! Become good friends, best friends; friends before lovers.

Being friends first could possible cause each of you less likely to hurt each other or be reckless with each other's feelings and emotions. What do you think?

Khrystianity

Don't be a woman that needs a man. Be that woman every man needs!

Chapter 4

Khrystianisms

Single Girl Gem~ Khrystian Tid-Bit Edition #88
When you can't see past what you want, you don't receive what you're WORTH!
You have to make them WORK for it!

A word to the wise: take mental notes. I've learned this attribute and often times I can be seen as quiet, reserved or shy. These quiet moments are my personal opportunity for gathering Khrystian Tid-bits, or Khrystianisms. I'm going to share some of my Khrystianity with you, my purpose for doing it, how it has helped me, and then supply a series of Khrystianisms to you as you read through this chapter.

Not everything requires a response or needs to be addressed. There is such a thing called mental notes. These are snapshots, if you will, of collective memories stored in your mind for later use. Ever heard the phrase: Silence is golden? You can do much more with silence than you could ever do with menial words. No need to address every issue, concern, situation or instance. Take some notes every now and then. Keep a mental photo album, if you will. There will come a grand time when all the stored information and memories will come in quite handy and for your ultimate benefit. Tread lightly. Speak easy. Take mental notes. The following are mine.

Placing expectations on someone we first meet will set you up for failure every time. I supposedly think like a man in more ways than I care to share, however one thing I know is certain: When you first meet someone, whether you're a man meeting a nice woman or a woman meeting a dapper man; please stop with the idiosyncrasies the moment you say hello to each other. This was brought back to my attention during one of my book club meetings.

We read the recommended read from the essence book club, The Conversation, by Hill Harper.

It's a book all about how black men and women can build loving and trusting relationships. Now, I know what you're about to say, "How can Hill Harper teach anyone about being in a healthy relationship when he's single and not qualified?"
You're absolutely right! How can he? Well, honestly; he's NOT doing any of the above mentioned. It's more of a series of his own quests to figure out what's wrong with him, or I should say, what he can do to help himself "look in the mirror" and figure out his own self worth and issues with relationships past, current and future. It's sort of like if I took my blog and interviewed a few people based on my topics and got it published. I published the blog but didn't interview anyone. Same difference.

  Any who, he writes sort of a self portrait of himself and now, because of it he's got all the world a-buzzing. I'll be the first to admit; when I picked up the book and read the first couple of pages I put the book down. I wasn't going to read it. I thought it was yet another one of "those". I figured, man…I know what he's about to say and how he's about to say it and why he's about to say it. After actually reading the entire book, my opinion didn't change. LOL It just didn't. BUT; I respect his book. I respect it enough to have read it. I respect it enough to discuss it at my book club, and I respect it enough to share in my book. One reason that I didn't turn a deaf ear to him was his perspective. I loved his perspective.

  He's a highly educated graduate of Brown as well as Harvard, a world traveler, a spiritually grounded single man, and if that's not enough; a man in search of truth and even more knowledge, major turn-ons in my opinion. Any who; I digress! The particular point I want to discuss at this time, and the entire reason I'm bringing up Hill Harper and his book are because of the statement I made earlier: Placing expectations on someone we first meet will set you up for failure every time.

During our book club discussion one of the ladies asked how we felt about Hill, on page nine of the book, telling a woman he was going to call her, and then not calling her until a month later. Okay. Most of the women in the book club were livid. One even said, "Unacceptable because the same way you begin a relationship, is the same way you will end a relationship." I kind of agree…but then that disputes Christianity and the ability to change in the twinkling of an eye. Careful what you say, and how quickly you let a judgment fly from your mouth. I was talking to myself there, but if the shoe fits for you too wear it.

Excuse me, I digressed again, back to the point- another lady said; "I would have been upset and had to explain to him that the behavior was unacceptable." Low and behold; I made my comment. "I'll have to check my sources to be accurate, but I'm pretty sure, he never gave her a date he was going to call. Why would you place expectations on this man you've just met an hour before-hand and may or may not see again?"

Why did I say that? They were all over me. Saying it was the "man" in me. Figuring I'm giving men excuses and ways out of being the ideal man for them. But honestly! You can't give these sorts of expectations. Alas! I found it on the bottom of page nine. He told her he'd call when she asked if he would, but never said a time. My opinion might be different, had he told her, "I'm going to call you tomorrow," and called a month later; but that wasn't the case. So, ladies and gentlemen-because we all do it-

Please stop with these expectations, rules and heavy stipulations. If you like someone when you first meet them that's GREAT. If you don't that's cool too, you are probably better off. I just feel when we place all these stipulations on the men and women we're dating; they're bound to fudge up. What's the saying, "rules are meant to be broken"; at least the unreasonable kind? The kind that makes the guy or girl think something is detrimentally wrong with you and they soon discover that your antics are the precise reason why you are single and will remain single for a very long time.

So he said he would like to see you soon? Who cares, life can't stop because he said he would like to see you soon. Get it? Keep "you" occupied. It encompasses spending time with self, enjoying self and having a great time with self. When you master self and learn to understand and appreciate yourself, it makes it easier to accept or enjoy the company of someone else, and not anxiously anticipate their arrival.

Just Because

Just because you slept with him, doesn't make him your man.

Just because you have a degree doesn't mean you have a job.

Just because you have a passport, doesn't mean you travel the world.

Just because you know scripture, read your bible nightly, sing in the church choir; it doesn't make you a CHRISTIAN.

Just because they made eye contact, doesn't mean they're interested.

Just because you work every day, doesn't mean you have money.

Just because you listen to a song on the radio, it doesn't make you a supporter.

Just because you vote in the election, it doesn't make you political.

Just because you work with children, the elderly, or overall well-being of people, doesn't mean you care.

Just because you graduated or passed a test doesn't make you a novice or an expert.

Just because you're married, it doesn't make you a housewife.

Just because you're in a relationship, it doesn't mean it's committed.

Just because people have eaten your food, it doesn't make you a good cook or a chef.

Just because you've heard of a person, it doesn't mean you know them.

Just because you have kids, it doesn't make you a good parent.

Just because you sing in a choir, it doesn't make you Whitney Houston.

Just because you argue a lot, it doesn't make you capable of being an attorney.

Just because you know a ton of people, it doesn't mean they know you.

Khrystian Tid-bit "A dog that brings a bone will carry a bone"
Think on these things! Someone that's always bringing you information: positive or negative is surely taking away information positively or negatively.
Let's just say: They STAY with a bone

Khrystian Tid-Bit It's SO easy to critique a finished product; talk to me when you start to CREATE! Everybody has something to say when things are complete, but no one is there in the trenches, through storm or rain, cloudy or clear days motivating, encouraging and for ding-dang-on-sure not creating. So if you're NOT creating....shut the hell up. Let us do what we do and you do what you do...NOTHING but criticize, complain and cripple.

Khrystian Tid-Bit We attract what we focus on. What's YOUR focus on? Power of attraction is a serious matter.

First Sunday Soul Session Khrystian Tid Bit
Stop looking for love. It's already yours. You have it. Take in what's around you and count all that surrounds you. Good love and God Bless

Khrystainism

Inspiration beyond what eyes have seen, ears have heard and eyes have felt.

Self-check!

It's never a bad time for yet another self-reflection moment, or as I like to say...self-check!

Have you reached the majority, if not ALL of your goals? Are you staying positive and promoting self awareness to any of your shortcomings in what's keeping you from your goals?

Have you maintained any daily evaluations or check lists? Have you done your part in actively pursuing purposeful relationships?

If not; it's NOT too late. Get up. Do it. Make it happen. Self-check! Let's get it

Life is too short, therefore you must: Live, Learn, Love, Laugh Out Loud, and Lose Track of Time

Write 'Em Down

Goals. How many of us have them? Hopefully, we all do. Take some time to write yours down. Watch how quickly that small affirmation can begin to offset and turn some things around for you. God gives us the desires of our heart, so surely what's for you is for YOU. (My mom's favorite thing to say) This world is BIG and GRAND. There's room enough for everyone's success. Ignite. Here's to chasing your DREAMS.

Khrystian Tid-bit Grow UP
Form your own opinions and fight your own battles! Stop relying on cliques, crews, da homies, your goons, or WHOMEVER else you try and claim. That's so middle school. Here's to the grown....and the SEXY

*Everything done in the dark does come to light. Be ready when it does.
*Sometimes you have to cut people OFF and you don't owe them an explanation. They're weeds in your flourishing garden.
*You can't teach what you don't know, and you can't lead where you don't go.
*Never marry anyone with little to give or nothing to lose.
*Apologizing just to say you were "the bigger person", does not make you the bigger person.
*Don't promise when you're happy, Don't reply when you're angry, and Don't decide when you're sad.
*Don't get confused between my personality and my attitude. My personality is who I am. My attitude depends on who you are.
*If a prostitute and a ruthless business man can fall in love...anyone can.
*Practice what you preach and preach ONLY what you practice.
*When older people try to tell you how bad your generation is, remind them who raised, trained and brought it up.

Khrystian Tid-bit
Live and Love UNCONDITIONALLY. Love is a learned behavior and life offers continual lessons. Grow, grow and grow...don't be stagnant. Life is too short not to use what you learn to do better daily.

Khrystianism
Never turn down a compliment or a gift. Why, you ask? Because you receive them from someone that has it in their spirit to give...say a gracious thank you and keep it moving.

Khrystian Tid-bit Say Hello to the Bad Guy
Live your life honestly, with integrity and independent of all negativity. It's the absolute truth that sometimes, especially if people aren't genuinely in a good place, they will attempt to throw salt, add shade, or even make-up in their sick minds criticism against you. However, if you adhere to staying honest, hold on to your integrity, and live in positivity keeping negative people and situations out of your life; no one will ever be able to say a bad thing about you.
They may want to or try to, but your life isn't fueled with any ammo for them so it and they are useless. Here's to GOOD living.

Khrystianism
Stay fierce! Don't operate in fear...be FEARLESS!

Khrystian Tid-bit
A condom is cheaper than child support and ABSTINENCE is FREE.

Khrystian Tid-Bits
You'll never get a whole heart with a full lie.
Don't allow fear to cheat you out of your dreams.
Be grateful that even when we can't put it into words he listens to our heart.
You'll know when you mean or have meant SOMETHING to someone; they tell the truth no matter how uncomfortable it is.
That moment when you figure out they or it wasn't what you thought it was...That moment is Vision.
Either find a way or make a way, which ever you choose...Make It happen.
The early bird gets the worm, but the second mouse gets the cheese. It's all about Perspective.
Happiness always sneaks in a door you did not think was open.

Permission for Obedience Khrystianism
God gives us the desires of our hearts...my prayer is the strength and OBEDIENCE to fulfill them ❤

Khrystian Tid-bit
Everyone should want someone that's a TREASURE, not someone random that just any old body can have! Wait for it...

No good can come from placing stipulations and harsh rules or regulations on your life. From the foods you eat, the company you keep, the places you travel or visit, to the career you have or even your every day health! Let me be absolutely crystal clear with this next statement: "SET REACHABLE GOALS AND ENJOY LIFE" This is a Khrystian tidbit, at best.

Now, I'll break it down even more. Some of us go to the extreme and cut off things that we enjoy cold turkey. Unless you're very God-given life depends on it; why do that? Here's where "reachable" comes into effect. If you want to stop eating a particular food, knowing that you enjoy it and in the past have eaten it every day; start off small. Cut back. Don't remove it totally. If you know your weight (over or under) is out of control; begin a slow to moderate work-out plan to alleviate and reduce the risk of shock or immediate pain.

Without going through a minimal list of examples, I think the key is to setting reachable, attainable goals are to not be so rigid with goals you set. It causes you to lose control or site of what you're truly trying to accomplish. It also could cause you to fall off the mark, and most often fail. Who really wants to fail? No one really wants to fail. So, I urge you to set reachable goals that are realistic, doable and that in the long run will make you viably happy with your outcome.

Remove those in your life that constantly withdraw from you spiritually, emotionally, mentally, physically, and financially. These people call themselves mad when your bank is closed. But you know what? If they want or desire to be in your life...they'll simply move, adapt or die! That's a little acronym I use to teach my students about survival of the fittest. Survival is part of life.

Move → Move on. Go elsewhere. Find someone else to withdraw from. You may continue to have them in your life, however; they won't withdraw from you. At least not too frequently.

Adapt → Learn that you won't continue to be used and abused and they'll respond accordingly and so will you.

Die → Stop being around you totally. They've discovered the jig is up and you are not their bank of opportunity and they can't infringe on you any longer. You don't want this type of person around you anyway. They don't love you and clearly don't like you either.

No deposit, no return. Actively make room for DEPOSITS in your life. It's essential to your health and soul.

Chapter 5

The Single Girl Holiday

~FEBRUARY~

The time of month for lovers and courting and romancing and flirting. Well, not so much for everyone. Then there's Valentine's Day, also known as, Single Awareness Day which is another name that often times we single girls refer to in discussions. For those of us that think of St. Valentine's Day as, Single Awareness Day, here's to hoping you don't drown in your own tears or bash all the couples of the world or hold your very own Waiting to Exhale Parties. I love you, even if you think not anyone else does.

February or Valentine's Day aren't the exclusive holidays that singles feel some sort of way, most holidays are in some way a reality check that you may not have a significant other in your life, but due to the very nature of this second month of the year. It's important that I devote a chapter to this season in my book, just as I do on my blog each year, in February.

There are some people, which includes couples, that have been brainwashed or, that's too harsh, so I'll say; persuaded to believe that Valentine's Day is this historical and national conspiracy that shouldn't be celebrated because they say, "we show love three hundred and sixty-five days a year," or, "there's no need to show love on just one particular day of the year."

That's bologna. Don't let someone feed you that line of bull and don't you agree to it. Now, granted, there are some people that celebrate no particular holiday or special occasion due to religious beliefs and whatnot. I'm not talking about that. I'm talking about the idiots that will celebrate a birthday, anniversary,

Martin Luther King Jr. Day, Fourth of July, April Fools Day, Thanksgiving and Christmas, but when Valentine's Day rolls around all of a sudden; they don't believe in celebrating holidays.
Get Real.

The truth of the matter is; no one ever said you don't show love all year. Valentine's, for those of us that aren't so literal or radical, is just a day designated to celebrate L.O.V.E. A day that everyone comes together at one time to recognize love. That love isn't just about husband/wife, boyfriend/girlfriend, but any and all love you share; whether for kids, grandparents, parents, siblings, friends and most importantly, God.

Of course we know you're thankful for family; however, like clockwork in November, we come together with our families in celebration of them all over food. Of course you're loved by family and friends everyday of your life, but on the day you were born, it's nice to join together eat, drink, and bear gifts; that you lasted yet another year and that we're able to enjoy you on the day you were born. Of course you value the hard work a secretary (um, excuse me...executive assistant) does; but it speaks volumes when you acknowledge them on the day set aside or know as Secretary's Day.

I say all of this just so people can get it together. It really grinds my gears that there are actually people that go overboard often times with their views and it's possibly because, especially in a new relationship; they just don't want to celebrate Valentine's with you. Give them another relationship where the mate is not going for that crock of potato soup and I bet you any kind of money they'll be singing a different tune; standing in a line to pick up flowers, candy, cards and a Teddy bear.

Keep in mind. Men only do what you allow them to do. Valentine's Day has gotten too commercial, but NEWSFLASH. Hasn't every American holiday we celebrate gotten too commercial? You damn near go into a Great Depression around Christmas time if you can't get your family everything they ask for. So get over it and tell anybody that tries to pump you with that line to get over it.

Of course, February fourteenth of any given year, is not the only time you should be showing love. You most definitely are supposed to show it every day; in every action, word and thought; but it is a day that everyone acknowledges love.

So get up. Love thy neighbor just as Christ loves you. Be blessed and be in love for God is love. Don't allow someone to remove the open celebration of love that you have always believed in because they have an idiosyncratic belief of how to celebrate or when to conveniently celebrate.

Here's a Valentine funny from several years back that I shared on my blog. The month started off cool. An off-again-on-again-always-M.I.A-he's-or-she's-just-not-that-into friend of mine, whose birthday I never forget because it's the day before Valentine's Day let me know that he was having a birthday dinner and wanted me to attend. Of course I would attend, the mere notion of him contacting me gave me butterflies, he's great eye-candy, kind of mysterious; considering I don't have concrete proof that he had a significant other, his elusiveness left much to the imagination. Leave that as it may, I went.

      I arrived fashionably late, calling to make sure it was still on, because I worked late that evening. I was invited to another engagement, so I figured if worse came to worse and he had a date, or his significant other present, I could easily shrug it off, go to the next event, and just be sad to myself in the car on the way; instead of attempting to pretend I had somewhere else to go. That's never an easy lie for me.

Upon arrival, and to my surprise, it was a small intimate party of him, myself and two of his co-workers both female. They seemed to have no interest in him and he in them; however, it was evident there wasn't any romance in the air for the two of us. I took it and rolled with it and enjoyed the night of food, Hurricane's and pictures. One of the other women at the party had been off and on the phone all night, so when a guy approached the table, it was no surprise it was a guest she had invited to join us. The birthday boy, my "friend", we'll just call him B was the only testosterone with our party. No problem for him, but not so much for us single women whom made up the remainder of the guests.

      The guy that arrived to the party, no question, was interested in me, and clearly just a friend to his invitee. I didn't want to be rude; but I was not interested. Since it was such a small setting though, you can't ignore or catch eyes with someone sitting across from you without intentionally always looking away, especially if he talks to you. For the purposes of this story, we'll call him "G"

Disclaimer I will say this; when asked specific relationship advice, I've always advised my friends to date openly. It doesn't mean sleep around. In fact, do not sleep with them. Do just as I implied...DATE! Go to a movie, be friendly, have dinner, play a board game. At the very least you have a nice friend to enjoy company with or even better, you can meet one of their great friends and have a complete love match. This is just my philosophy. It doesn't work for everyone, but for me it does, has and will. You also have to take caution and pay attention to the other parties' feelings. You never want to intentionally hurt someone or play games with their emotions***

Now back to the story: "G" was a cool cat. He had a pleasant conversation at the table and it wasn't like it was just he and I talking. I never felt obligated on anything. I was just keeping it friendly with the group. Well B, true to form, asks me what other big plans did I have for the night, he said he asked because I was the biggest party girl he knew, and this had to just be a beginning for me. He was right, but talk about putting me on blast.

Why did B start that conversation because as soon as he did "G" took the reins and continued asking me details about where I would go. The entire table "jokingly" said they were going. I say jokingly, because they were just talking big and had no real intentions of going anywhere but home. However, "G" was serious. He actually got into his car and followed me to the next location.

Once at the next party, I got out of the car and asked him what he was doing. I didn't want to come across as upset as I was, because, let's face it, I just met the man less than thirty minutes ago, but I was wondering. I didn't have any fear because I thought to myself; well I did set myself up. I told him he was welcome. You know in the same joking way I was telling everyone else at dinner.

He entered the party with me, and low and behold, because I never bring guys out with me, all my friends were kind of stunned that I showed up with a dude out of nowhere that I hadn't been dating, and to a friend's birthday party no doubt. We drank more, laughed more, ate more, and just talked more. I figured he's not so bad a guy obviously or he wouldn't have been at B's dinner in the first place.

However, it still seems a little weird that I was partying with a person I had only just met. By the end of the night, one of my bestie's whom had a little too much to drink couldn't drive home, literally not a good situation. Another mutual friend agreed to make sure she made it home safely. "G" decided since he didn't know the person taking my bestie home, and I drank so much as well, he needed to follow to at least his exit which was three exits north of me and get my number to double check that I made it home safely. I agreed. I figured he was being a gentlemen and a good Samaritan. After all, we were indeed a good hour from our neck of the woods.

As we drove I give a check and go to him once we get close to his exit. He calls me to hear assurance that I'm okay. I say yes and we speak for a little bit longer. Next thing I know, "G" doesn't get off at his exit. He keeps driving. I never say a word, but in my mind, I'm almost scared. It was well after two in the morning. He's still behind me, until right before my exit, and he comes off the freeway with me. Now I'm more than slightly worried.

Long story short. He follows me home. Yes, this is terrifying, considering I just met this man only about two hours prior. He's supposed to be on his merry way home, but then takes my exit and then parks in my driveway.

I rush out of the car, and before he can get out good, I'm barking what the hell are you doing? Not caring in the slightest, since I'm home now, the manner in which I came off. He says, "I know this is weird, but I wanted to make sure you made it safe and if you don't mind, could I use your restroom?" My immediate thoughts were, HELL NO!

I'm thinking this is the type of thing you see on TV, some movie, or the news. Girl goes out for the night, comes home and family finds her dead in her own bed, or driveway or some other freaky-scary-tragic ending. I tell him, I appreciate the sentiment of following me home, but it is way too late for him to think it's appropriate to enter my house and use the restroom. He obliges (whew) and comes over to kiss me on the cheek thanking me for the night. WEIRD! I agree.

This all happened February thirteenth and yes, freakishly, it was Friday the Thirteenth! Go figure. So of course the next day is Valentine's Day. This year I had no official valentine, and I was fine with it. My bestie and I decided that dinner and movies would be great. Neither of us had a Valentine, so we made plans to go and see a scary movie.

Earlier that day as I was completing my cupid shopping, a self-made ritual of buying little cutsie gifts or flowers for specific family members, I get a call from none other than "G". Wow. I think to myself and at first, want to ignore, but then think nicely and go ahead and answer.

"Hey! How's it going?" He asks. "Good, just getting some errands run." I say. "So you still don't have a valentine, huh?" He asks based on our conversation at the party the night before. "Nope, my friend and I are going to do dinner and a movie. We're each other's valentine." "How about we go catch a movie or something. I'd like for you to be my valentine." He says. "Well I just told you what I was doing." I tell him. "Maybe I could meet you two or something. I won't take up your whole night; just meet you at the movies." He chimes.

Ordinarily I would have been annoyed with him, but I have to explain to you so that you understand, at this point, one of my major resolutions for the New Year had been to be a better, more understanding person of another person's feelings. I had long since been told, I wasn't a very friendly or empathetic and I was genuinely trying to be better. I don't want to say

"G" sounded pitiful, but something about the way he sounded soften me to agree and say that would be fine.

Needless to say, being a better person in this moment sucks. I should have stuck with my old ways and said Hell to the no. We learn though. The night wasn't fun, he almost had us late for the movie, I had to leave out , and show him where we were sitting because he arrived late, causing me to miss some of the plot, I got his ticket for him previously because it would have been sold out, had he waited, he didn't buy popcorn or drinks, nor did he apologize for being late, he talked through the movie, he didn't get me a valentine...now, maybe I would have chalked all of that up, but then his ass tried to kiss me at the end of the night as if it was an actual date after he didn't behave as if it were one.

I drew the line there and refused any nice other omissions on my part. What kind of valentine doesn't give you at least the convenience store bought chocolates and bear, with the generic card and maybe plastic flowers? Sorry, not a cool Valentine buddy. Good thing I have great girlfriends and family. At dinner earlier, my friends and I had a small exchange of meaningless gifts, trinkets and cards.

The next day I ignored his calls. I finally answered later in the evening. He asked me out again. I said no. He said he would have to wait until another party or outing to see me, I told him no, and that I wasn't interested in him. He asked if he could call me at another time, thinking maybe I had just gotten out of a relationship. I told him no. He didn't know it but my last relationship had been over more than a year prior.

I just wasn't interested in dating him. He told me that was harsh. I said, I was just being honest. He said maybe he'd call to just be friends. I said don't bother and told him to have a good day. He texted me anyway. I ignored until it ended.

Valentine's 101

I've had some great Valentine's dates, as I'm sure you have as well. As you could tell from the story there are a few ways you can go terribly wrong when it comes to Valentine's Day fun and surprises.

First things first; don't just go on a date, just for the sake of having a date. It's not worth it in the end. Stay patient. Also don't bother getting caught up in the hype of the holiday and turn bitter because of what you see around you. Yea, we know you just love and show love to your people every day, all day. Lighten up, it's just another one of those memorable occasions to celebrate, mmkay?!

Of course traditionally, the original culprits are flowers, candy, teddy bears, jewelry, etc.

But here are a few of my easy-breezy go-to ideas specifically for Valentine's gifts and treats:

1. Undergarments (socks, underwear, undershirts)

2. Pajamas/Various sleepwears

3. Chocolates

4. Novelty gifts (chocolate-covered something, grooming, and electronics, other...umm...toys)

Get creative

1. Coupons are always fun

2. Calendars with themed months are a hit

3. Personalized photos are easy

4. Cooking/Painting/Dance/Etc. classes are exciting

     Most importantly, get a flattering card that expresses your relationship. If you can't buy one, make one. You can do this by hand or electronically. Computers do everything and Google is our friend.

     I love, love, love to bake cookies, brownies, a cake, or cupcakes too and decorate them in reds, pinks, and whites. It just adds a little something to the festivities. Whatever you choose or decide, make it personal. Have fun and enjoy the moments you create with your Loved Ones.

Xoxo

Chapter 6
Random Rants

When it seems as if you're down to nothing, know that God is up to something.

Stop using your body as if it's a congenial welcome mat at the door of Stop n' Go. You should have much more to offer this world than a piece of ass. If your personal relationships aren't lasting more than six months…SELF CHECK!

If you're ever feeling so low that you just want to crawl under the covers and hide from the rest of the world. Remember that if God brought you to it, he'll get you through it.

The best way to show that you have dignity, class, poise and savvy, both professionally and personally, is to act in that manner at all times. Those are qualities others see shining from you. You shouldn't have to announce those attributes.

It has been said that character is the way you behave when no one is watching. Often times we put on a grand, magnificent and entertaining "show' in front of our loved ones. Sooner or later you show your true colors. Be yourself, even when you think no one likes the real you.

Stop letting others determine your value and self-esteem. Love yourself first and others will follow suit. Remove yourself from all negativity. Wake up in the mornings thinking of how you can empower others. Through empowering others you will fully empower yourself.

Khrystian Tid-Bit R.E.S.P.E.C.T.

Now-a-days kids aren't taught it and most adults don't show it. It's a sad thing to be writing about but it's a necessary evil that must be discussed. To people, I might say something like, "If your parents didn't or won't teach you, I'll teach you about respect."

It starts with us, the supposed "adults". We're the ones the kids look up to for guidance and as role models. It doesn't matter if you want to be one or not. Your positive or negative actions are watched and it's especially sad, if you have children and have no regard for your behavior around them. Being a parent is a RESPONSIBILITY. Any doofus can produce a child, but it takes responsible individuals to raise a child and be a parent.

The dictionary defines respect as: an act of giving particular attention: thoughtfulness: high or extraordinary regard: value: the quality or state of being esteemed: expressions of high or special regard or reverence

One particular rule I was taught is to respect my elders. When I was a child it was super easy to decipher an elder. Now that I'm older the line has become fuzzy. Not to mention the fact, that most elders, now-a-days, aren't themselves respectable. I believe, however, the underlying theme is still prevalent. Just show consideration to people, their space, opinions, and feelings. Respect is earned, not deserved.

It's simple and if you didn't care about anything I just wrote in the prior lines, please take heed to these next gems of wisdom: Don't do and/or say things that you have to consistently apologize for. Live your life unapologetically and not because you're rude and pompous, but because you're living on purpose with consideration to those around you.

Why ask Why?

Why do people continually ask the questions they already know the answer to? "Do you think he has somebody? We only text or email, and he never answers *my* call."
Umm, yes!

"Is this dress too short? I feel a breeze!"
Yes!

"Do I seem desperate always jumping into bad relationships?"
Heck yes!

"I know for sure he only wants sex from me, that's evident. It's all we talk about. What you think?"
Do you really have to ask? YES!

"I hate my job, and this lady just called me about a transfer. It's totally a different job with better benefits. What you think?"
DUH!

"He's changed. He doesn't even act the same and we are never intimate anymore. Do you think he's messing around?"

    I'm not even going to say anything else, because you already know my answer. I mean really. Don't be silly. You already know what sound advice is. You already know if it walks like a duck and quacks like a duck, it's a ding-dang-on duck. I suppose some folks just want reassurance, but sincerely, like for real, for real…get it together.

Chapter 7
Those Awkward Moments

Cat's Meow

Cat's Meow, always, somehow
A woman's pleasure can be described as this
The love I'm speaking of brings ultimate bliss
Sisters, you know what I'm saying
After 48 hours it'll have you on your knees still praying
The passion was like a shot of penicillin injected
As your body reacted and didn't reject it
With all your might u tried to hold it in
The feel the touch let's face it you fought but did not win
From that one long stroke
You purred a long note
Cat's meow, always somehow
Caressing your hair
Child I'm talking about everywhere
U want to hide your face
Don't just sit back and embrace
It's all so simple
Like a smile without dimples
Cat's meow always somehow, somehow always, always somehow
And the feeling begins right now

I wrote that poem at the age of seventeen. What did I know? What could I have possibly known about anybody's cat's meow? I was a seventeen year old proud virgin and hadn't even had my first kiss. I'm not too old or too proud to admit that. I didn't get my first tongue kiss until the spring of my senior year in high school.

The kiss was atrociously sloppy, wet, and overall disgusting. I had no idea what I was doing. The guy was a year younger than me and had, what I thought, was experience, but now looking back; he couldn't have been too experienced, either; unless, he was just a bad kisser. Needless to say, the kisses I've experienced since then, even a kiss on the cheek from my grandmother, have been more endearing than that first kiss.

This was the beginning of my cases of the awkward moments. A string of awkward moments were close behind that. Moments that I wish I could take back. Moments I wish I could get in the bed, pull the covers over my head and hide from the world. Moments that could be laughable if they weren't at my expense.

I decided to enter this poem into a poetry contest. I consequently won an opportunity to get published on Poetry.com. I didn't at the time truly understand the magnitude of my words, but now looking back I laugh. I had no idea about a cat's meow, but I sure did have imagination and a way with simple words.

Cases of that awkward moment, we all have them. Awkward, uncomfortable, inconvenient and downright embarrassing moments are all too common and happen all too often. The absolute funniest thing is that it does, in fact, only last a moment. They occur in the blink of an eye, but somehow it can be, well, awkward.

Here are some I'm listing and detailing. Some

are true stories, most are false from my imagination that could have happened, but you may find one or all you can relate to.

Those awkward moments:

1. Driving in your car on the way somewhere and you realize you're a week early.

2. You're trying to end a conversation and the other person won't stop talking.

3. You ask a woman how far along she is only to find out she's not pregnant (oops).

4. You're mad you didn't get a reply to your text...that you actually never sent.

5. You text the right message to the wrong person.

6. Someone is waiting with their hand up for a high-five but you're not looking (Do people still give hi-fives?)

7. You've already said "what?" three times and yet you still have no idea what the person said so you just agree to move the conversation along.

8. You're behind a slow walker or car and there's no way around them.

9. You have all the attention in the world....from the wrong person.

10. Someone is giving you answers to questions you did not ask.

11. Walking past a parked car; you stop and look at yourself in the window, and there's still people in the car.

12. Your stomach gurgles loudly during the quietest situations/place.

13. Halfway through an argument you realize you're wrong.

14. On the dance floor when you're minding your own business and someone (you don't want) comes up behind you ruining your groove.

15. Your ex-boyfriend points out to you the long strand of hair growing from your face.

That Awkward Moment # 16
Do not discount the underdogs, the geeks, the so-called losers, the nerds, the unpopular; those are often the very people in life that actually have a terrific turnaround through life. It's the classic geek to chic scenario or Frog to Prince Syndrome, never discredit someone whom "seems" to not be the "hot ticket" at the time.

That Awkward Moment #17
You see your ex out and about, hold a conversation to catch up, and exchange numbers knowing you won't be in touch. Pleasantries!

That Awkward Moment #18

You realize being sentimental about what you believe to be their genuine actions and original words is pointless because it's all a part of their ammo used to pick-up any and everybody.

That Awkward Moment #19
Someone spends more time on Facebook, Twitter, Instagram, texting, emailing, Googling, or just plain old staring at the screen of their phone when they're actually supposed to be spending "time" with you.

Awkward Relationship Behavior
It's always important when entering and maintaining a healthy relationship for you to be free to be you and have the confidence to openly express yourself to your mate. You should not have to feel like you're "performing" in your relationships; being someone you're not or holding your feelings in, especially not in your intimate or personal relationships.

   You should always feel comfortable to be yourself with and around your mate! That's the benefit of having someone that loves you; they accept you. If you're in a relationship and you're ostracized for being yourself, you should rethink that commitment. I'm just saying.

For instance- Awkward Relationship Behavior #1:
You're being flirty with your mate or initiating some sort of intimacy, whether it's a private conversation or hand-holding but instead of following your lead, making you feel safe and secure by engaging with you they accuse you of being inebriated! You ask a serious question or emotionally put yourself out there and they automatically deduce your behavior to having one too

many drinks or say, "what's gotten into you?" or "you're acting weird/strange!"

I think something's wrong there. What do you think? I think your mate will never initiate again. I think you've shut down or alienated a part of your mate they were attempting to unveil and share. This may cause concealment.

This then begins a vicious domino effect. The mate that's "shot down" the other, at a later date, is now wondering why they aren't open with their feelings. Why aren't they affectionate? Why don't they initiate? Is that not awkward relationship behavior? Don't diminish someone's feelings. Even if it seems out of character for your mate; clearly, they are comfortable with you. Remember we discussed the "silly" side? They say love makes people do strange, different, and wonderful-no less-things. You stifle your relationships growth when you point out what someone is doing, especially if it's not harming you. My goodness; it's flirting or initiating intimacy, how dare your mate want to flirt with you or be intimate? What monsters they must be? Think twice before you belittle your mate's advances, initiation and affection.

Chapter 8

As The World Turns (in Real Life)…Episodes

Khrystian Tidbit
Don't start no shit, won't be no shit! (Stuff my family says)
…and if you do start some shit. Do NOT apologize. Loser! (That's stuff I say)

As the World Turns (in real life)...
"After reading your blog, I decided to write you. I am coming to you because you may have the answers or insight on a few challenges that I am having at this time. I cannot discuss this with my friends because I do not want them in my business at all. I have to have closure and peace with this whole situation. Playing with a fool will make you foolish. I have been embarrassed for weeks and refuse to feel this way another day.

He got my number from Facebook. I am only communicating with him right now only because he owes me money. He supposedly lost his wallet. After that someone used his checking card. Then his bank froze his account to investigate. Like a dumb ass I loaned him money. I know it may sound crazy and I can't tell you that it all makes sense. He has paid me back half of what he owes. He keeps making excuses saying he will return the money tomorrow, like every day...I had a law enforcement friend check him out. I was advised that he has a history of fraud. I do not know him and I feel horrible that I allowed him for a brief time in my world.

I do not know him very well. All I know is that he is a habitual liar. In your personal opinion should I leave the balance that he owes me alone? Is he a criminal? There is so much I don't know. Is he dangerous? I do not like the fact that he knows where I live. My daughter and I live here and I almost want to move because of this."

   Time and time it's been said...desperate times call for desperate measures. Of course, I don't know the extent to this so-called relationship and I never truly will... frankly; it doesn't matter...but I can tell you safety is number one.

Safety is what should have caused you not to engage in a relationship of any kind with someone you don't know that "psycho-ly" got your number from Facebook (rule numero Uno!) *Safety* would have told you; if you don't know him very well he should NOT be at your home and most definitely in any location where your child dwells. *Safety* should have propelled you to find out those latter questions you asked of yourself and law enforcement friend about him in the beginning and not now that he owes you money. *Safety* is what should have been your biggest knock in the head to not loan someone you don't know any money whatsoever.

If *safety* is now all of a sudden your concern...leave the balance as is! I won't continue to berate you; for as you said; you've "been embarrassed for weeks", but I will emphasize- Live and Learn! Pick up and learn from your mistakes- next time, hang up the phone as soon as someone says they got your number from Facebook! At least use a reputable source like match.com or something! They do reference checks!! LOL!

As the World Turns (in real-life)... Episode 2
"Hey! How are you doing? I hope you are doing great and staying blessed. I have been trying to get in touch with someone and they're not returning my calls. They owe me money and won't call me or send me my check. Facebook... erased. And emails or calls no response. All this what happened, didn't only happen to me!! It happens to a lot of other girls and I really can't get in touch or make contact, so I was wondering if you could

advise me? Please let me know and God bless you! I really appreciate it. Ciao ciao"

So often we become victims of our kind hearts and circumstances. I think the most important thing to do, is going to either- follow through legally, that is provided you have proper evidence that money is owed to you, continue contacting via web, ask the other girls how they handled the situation, or charge it as a learning lesson. The lesson: ALWAYS have signed documents, contracts, agreements, whatever, when conducting business. Not only that; don't do work or complete work in full until you're either paid partially or on the agreed upon terms. Set deadlines. Set parameters.

Business is business. So often people jump into a so-called "business" situation not really understanding what they are doing or whom they're entering into that "business" with. As once said on Jerry Maguire, "It's not show-friends, it's show-business." Treat it as such. Going into a business arrangement with someone and not having a contract is like working for someone where you have to pay their bills and when it's time for you to get paid; you actually expect them to have money to pay you! Umm, hello?! You just had to PAY *their* bills! It just doesn't happen...not realistically anyway!

However, God's not sleep. He takes care of his children. Maybe he needed the money more than you; maybe God has something much better in store for you! Whatever the situation; count it ALL joy! It'll all work itself out in due time!

As The World Turns (in real life)...Episode 3

"I met this guy through a mutual friend one day at his house and through talking; I began explaining to him that I was looking for a new place. I'd had an issue with my landlord and was in the process of court matters. He, himself, had a nice place and explained to me that he had another lease property around town. Not only that; he said I seemed like a cool person, someone he could be friends with while he was in town and maybe check out the new Batman movie. I agreed and gave him my number, not sure if he was capable of being friends, but hopeful! At first I was slightly leery because he seemed to want to talk alone and upstairs in his bedroom.

I'm fresh out of a relationship and not really comfortable enough to move on just yet, so I asked a close friend of mine, who happens to be his ex-girlfriends friend, what she knew of him and if he was capable of solely having a friendship. However, now that we've exchanged numbers he contacts me late at night saying he wants to see me, asking me what I'm doing, or trying to get me to come over and watch movies. He assures me with rather slick comments that he could have any women he wanted if he was just trying to get with someone, but he feels that I seem like someone that can be cool to hang out with.

His actions (the late night texts/calls) seem to be questionable. Not to mention the fact I've kind of expressed to him reservations of hanging out with him considering my friend being so close with his ex. Something just doesn't feel right. Not only that; he's told me he's won't accept my reason for not wanting to hang with him and that he's not letting me off that easy!

I'm beginning to get turn-offed and creeped out by him. I'm not sure what his motivation is for the constant calling and texting especially since we haven't known each other long at all. It's gotten so bad he's contacting me while I'm at work. I'm thinking, if all you want is a friend, and as you said, clearly could have anybody to sleep with; why are you making such a big deal about hanging out with me and, at this point, creeping me out with your incessant phone calls. The last text I got from him was something in the neighborhood of: 'I was just trying to help you out with your situation and be a friend, you seem cool. Have a good weekend.' What do you think?"

It's pretty clear: You started off very interested or you wouldn't have exchanged numbers! Formulate your opinion based off your encounters with him. You're an adult. As adults, we have discernment enough to know when something feels right or wrong. Talking it out with others may just be your way of seeking further approval to hang out with him.

If that's the case; you don't need approval- DO IT! If nothing else, you have someone to "hang out" with from time to time that could very well lead to a great romance! If your concern is the time of day he contacts you- TELL HIM! If he is trying to be "a friend" he'll respect your request of an earlier call time. If it is concern for your friends' opinion, you do not need it.

No one knows what you want more than you. If you're truly not interested-MOVE AROUND! But it's never cool to lead someone on by entertaining something you have no desire for. You don't want to have him thinking his actions are cool with you or charming all the while you're laughing at him with your friend and actually saying he's creeping you out! Be straight up! Be adult!

As The World Turns (in real life)… Episode 4
"I've been living with this man for two years. I love him very much but here lately I've found bank statements from out of town ATM's on days and nights he was supposed to be at work. My EZ tag has to be added to or charged double time, he also has a number on his cell phone bill, that I pay, where he is talking all day and night for extensive amounts of time. He gets upset with me for any little thing, especially if I question him about about anything and lately he sleeps on the couch. Our work schedules have been crucial, but I feel there's something else. I prepared and had his entire family over, including out of towners for holiday dinner and spent a lot of money on their Christmas gifts. I called the number in his phone that's listed as a male name, but when I called a female answered. On top of all this; our sex life has declined drastically."

I had enough with reading and it was just too much information on that note. You have ALL the evidence in the world to convict and yet you want my answer....a deliberation! Come on! There's no easy way to say that he's seeing someone else. I don't mean to sound curt; but he's probably been buying time through the holidays to either keep his little honey dip around, and/or planning some sort of breakup with one of you.

Clearly he can't continue on the way he's going...or perhaps he can; if you'll allow it! No need to go through his phone (although I can understand why if he's constantly lying AND you're paying the bill) but it would seem as though he didn't want to abruptly change holiday plans, you're making it real EASY for him to do as he pleases: footing the bill, allowing him to sleep on the couch (what is that?!). Hey, I'm not advocating fornication, pre-marital sex, and such and such, but I will say; you already bought the cow, so why would you not drink the milk by accepting his downright rude behavior.

     I understand you began saying you love him...but he's NOT displaying love and certainly not with you! Take it from me...the "new" male name in the phone is the woman he's seeing! Let them live happily ever after...he'll see the grass isn't greener on the other side. Whether the other woman knows about you or not...HE should know better and HE'S as wrong as two left shoes! First, for not being man enough to tell you he wasn't happy with you and second, for abusing your kind, giving, supportive nature then third, for being a giglo and fourth, for being all of that wrapped into an arrogant asshole. How dare he assume an attitude with you?!

     Move on girl. That's not love...he's using the hell out of you!

As The World Turns (in real life)… Episode 5
"Difference Between Fiction and Reality"
Here's a story that a bitter woman told. After you read the fiction story that the bitter woman told, I'll give you the eyes-wide open REALITY!
Bitter Woman: *I'm at a graduation party and a woman (a hometown associate) came up to me asking how I'd been since the divorce. I answered great! Then she asked how my ex-husband was. I then replied, well you*

should know! You go to dinners and movies with him and his new woman. The associate looks puzzled since I've now called her out. I continue and say, my daughter's dad is fine.
The associate then goes on to tell me. She's heard he's doing quite well and has gotten newly engaged, and he's been looking at houses with his new woman. I then tell my associate, I hadn't heard of that and I'm pretty sure if I wanted my marriage, I could still have it back.

Here's the REALITY

The bitter woman saw her hometown associates (two of them) out last year (several months back) with her ex-husband and a woman. She previously spoke and held a conversation with the associates before she saw that her associates were clearly at the movies with her ex-husband and his new boo on some type of couples outing. Had she known before she spoke to the associates...her bitterness more than likely would have prevented her from speaking to them?

  Fast forward to the graduation party the bitter woman attends; she now, sees one of the culprits, er... I mean associates, and thinks it's a perfect opportunity to "find out" from a third-party what's up with her ex-husband, since obviously the associate is "friends" enough to go to dinner and a movie with her ex-husband's new woman.

  The bitter woman speaks to the associate. The associate speaks and asks the bitter woman how has everyone (meaning mother and child) been and adjusting since the divorce. The bitter woman says, I'm great, but you should know how my ex-husband is doing since you hang out, going to dinner and movies with him and his new boo all the time, but anyway...his daughter is good too!

      The associate looks puzzled because her intentions were to speak and this bitter broad has opened an entire new can of worms that she couldn't care less about because she has her own husband and two kids to worry with. Why would she be concerned about a divorced bitter woman and her EX-husband!
 The associate then says she doesn't know about all of that. Yes we've been around each other once but the last thing I've heard is that they're looking at houses, and talking engagements so they must be still together and happy.

      Upset at the twist of events and the fact that the taste was just slapped out of her mouth since that's not the answer or reaction she was looking for from the associate; the bitter woman's only outlet is to go into quick defense mode and say in one swift comment, I don't know about any of that...I'm pretty sure if I wanted my marriage I could have it back.

      One story makes sense, adds up, and goes in a logical order while the other story is sporadic, unclear, and clearly not thought through. One story makes sense while the other does not. One story has a clear motive by someone and shows a self-serving purpose, while the other sounds absurd! One even oozes with a bitter, tart smell...but hey; you decide.

xoxo,
Live in love, not hate. Stay in your lanes sweetie pies...you might get crashed and burned.

Chapter 9
Gifts That Keep Giving

Unsolicited Advice

You know those times someone, anyone, gives you advice that you didn't ask for? Yes, referring back to those awkward moments where you realize you didn't ask for an opinion, but one was given to you anyway and without your consent. It happens to everyone, but especially us single girls. I'm joining the club and giving it away as well.

Careful whom you call your friends
They are talking about you behind your back and don't have the courage to tell you to your face. They will mask an underhanded compliment with a smile or joke. You remember the time everyone laughed and you were lost? Yes, they were talking about you and that's not what friends do.

They don't know how to love you
You know a person loves you when you're not questioning it. Actions speak louder than that void "love" word they're giving. Contrary to popular belief love does not hurt. It feels good and you want that feeling all the time once you get it.

You can do it
Sure, it's cliché, but it's the truth. It won't always come when you want it but the change will come. You can make it happen; you have the capability one way or another.

There's nothing "cute" about being known for having a bad attitude or a negative disposition
Get your life. It's too short. We all have our crosses to bear, but nothing is more precious than time. It's our worst enemy and once you lose it; you never get it back. Don't waste it away with negativity and stupidity.

*Shower others for their good work and correct them

when it's not up to par*
This includes tipping servers.
Don't be so proud that you miss out on good things
Help is normally a phone call away and with technology in this day and age Google search away. Ask, or at the very least listen and take nuggets that people give out because in this day and age they're few and far between so if someone is giving them be sure to take it.
Not everyone is for you
Pray for discernment. Ask for wisdom.
If you have to suck it in or lay across the bed to zip up they are too tight to wear to any civilized event
Yes, we can see what you feel. There's nothing wrong with self-esteem but there's something wrong with those pants.
Don't lead people on
If you know you're not hiring them, let them know via email, phone call, letter, your assistant, or something. If you don't want to be serious with them, tell them. If they choose to stay after that, at least you've said your peace. Practice being upfront with people.

Bridal Shower Gift Ideas

Love is in the air, somewhere. I'm a confessed bonafide procrastinator. I'm not proud, but it's my story. As they say, "It is what it is." Very rarely am I able to think of, order, and get shipped anything personalized; so with that being said I'm putting together a list of great bridal shower ideas that are sure-fire lovely gifts for the intended receiver to ensure a picture with them, or at the very least a thank you card. You could very

easily personalize some of them or not, but they're nice, inexpensive, great and simple ideas.
- Linen napkins and napkin rings
- Picture frame
- Champagne/Martini glasses
- Vase
- Blender/Mixer
- Coffee maker
- Bundt pan
- Lingerie
- Cookbook
- Cocktail guidebook
- Bathing suit for the honeymoon
- Wine/Stopper/Holder
- Embroidered robe
- Breakfast-in-bed tray
- Theater tickets
- Luggage
- Beach towels and a beach bag
- His/Her massage
- Gift certificates (you can NEVER go wrong)

The Art of the Re-Gift

It's one of those things that everybody does, but nobody talks about. Holidays, birthdays, and special occasions usually involve gift-giving of some sort. Most times re-gifting is planned, other times not so much. It begins with a gift. One person receives a gift, has a gift, or has something in their possession that they can't or won't use and so would serve as a greater gift to someone else. At least one can only hope it works out for them instead.

It doesn't necessarily mean the original recipient thought the gift sucked, it just means it doesn't work for them or they can't use it. It also doesn't mean the person receiving the gift sucks; it just means they are more suited for the unknown gift.

      Heck, and to keep it really real, as I do; you may just not have it to do at the time and the best solution for you will be to re-gift. Whatever you're initial reasoning, it's all about the effort you place into re-gifting. Understanding the art of re-gifting is important because it is a special craft.

There are specific cases when re-gifting absolutely works:

1. The person you're re-gifting does not know it was a previous gift, otherwise known as hand-me-down.
2. The gift is perfect for them. Their personality, size, or it's just plain ole' something they wanted.
3. The gift is in perfect condition. Original tags attached, fresh, preferably perfectly packaged.
4. It's useful. Although it may not have worked for you, it's perfect for them.
5. Accompany the gift with a thoughtful, new card. It ties it all together.

Here's when re-gifting goes terribly wrong. ABORT MISSION!

1. The person receiving the gift knows it's a re-gift and they were presumed to believe it was original.
2. It was something you didn't want, and now they don't want it because it's out of date or season, not their personality, size or style.
3. It's been used, missing pieces, fragrance low, tags are worn so bad they are soft or there are stains.

4. Original names are still on the gift. Please double check the gift. That's just common courtesy.

      All in all, there's nothing blatantly wrong with re-gifting in my opinion however, there's a certain decorum you must practice when doing so. The key is awareness in making sure the gift will suit your receiver and you understand the gift must be in great condition, examine it, and then bag it. Place yourself in the receiver's shoes.

      Now to be clear: It's a total other story if you're giving away something. That's not a gift. When you give away something; you don't have to wrap it, because it's not a surprise, and the person receiving it more than likely is clearly aware that it may or may not have been used.

Here are some lovely ideas for re-gifting:

*Electronics
*Fragrance
*Houseware
*Equipment
*Travel vouchers
*Movie Passes
*Gift cards

It may never happen, especially if you follow the art of the re-gift however, just as insurance here's what to do when you've been caught re-gifting:

1. Acknowledgement- Do not insult the person's intelligence or pretend like it never happened. Express to them exactly why you would give them the re-gift:

2. Profess- "It's perfect for you." "When first I got this, I knew you had to have it." Any variation to the above will do. As long as you're honest and sincere, they should understand. If you're gifting them, you'd think

they know you.
3. Embrace-Throw a hug in for good measure, and for goodness sake make sure the card is thoughtful and the bagging or wrapping is impeccable.

Last Minute Gift Ideas!

Many of us need those last minute gift ideas and/or stocking stuffers during Christmas time, and by last minute, I don't mean Christmas Day; I mean the week of Christmas, or the day of the party! Here are some ideas I've come up with. These can be for family, friends or associates. Add to my list or not.
1. Cd/DVD/Book combinations
For instance: Sex And The City book, movie and soundtrack;
The Help, He's Just Not That Into You, Waiting to Exhale, Color Purple, etc
2. Gift Cards
Anywhere THEY love, not YOU love! LOL!
Restaurants, book stores, specialty stores, iTunes, etc
3. Home Decor or Electronics
This requires a relationship of enhancement. The gift should be something they genuinely could use
4. Wine/glasses/cork
Nothing better than a tasty wine! A fun either personalized wine glass or a nice set conducive to that wine selection and an even more fun cork
5. Accessories
Glasses, hats, scarves/glove set, JEWELRY, etc
6. Make-up
Or it's accessories

Chapter 10
Scenes in Dating

...It happened one night

Every now and again you have an incredible day that turns into the evening. Well let me rephrase that statement; you have a day whether it's good or bad, and so you pull over from a long drive to sit at a bar on the way home from this day. This bar can be as simple as a restaurant bar, it's nothing fancy, in fact; it's not even planned. You're in your work clothes, or perhaps worse. Hey, stranger things can happen, but every now and then, this night happens.

Traffic is horrible. You pull over to let the traffic pass because you have a long road ahead. While sitting, minding your own business, someone, someone attractive, introduces themselves to you. A conversation ensues and you enjoy each others' company profusely. One drink turns into another, and another, and another, followed by a great dinner.

You find that you enjoy each others' company so much, neither of you are quite ready for the night to end so you move to a new location, a game room. You further enjoy each other by gaming and drinking. Before you know it, it's 1:30 in the morning and you both need to go to work in a few hours.

Your goodbyes are said but not for long because you call each other to talk to one another until you can't control what comes out of your mouth or keep your eyes open. You wake to a, "*Good morning, I hope you have a great day*" text. Does that sounds like a cool first date? Maybe, however; it's really the beginning of a beautiful, unexpected friendship to me, or is it? ...it happened one night.

Dating 237

Dating can be great with the right person as we all know. It's hard out here. I'm not going to lie to you. I can't sugar-coat the truth. I won't even paint a pretty picture! It is down-right rough. All of you married and engaged or serious relationship people, let's give a toast to you. Although in your own right, you have a ton of hurdles to get over and plenty of mountains to climb. You're doing it with (hopefully) one person; (hopefully) exclusively and for that a round of applause is due.

These days guys and women can be so crude, rude, and straight-up out of line. They say any little old thing that pops up in their head. *Case in point "I wonder if you taste as good as you look." I mean, who in the hell says that? Folks out here dating and starving for your body, that's who. That's all they want. They're not interested in getting to know you, your family, your goals, or your level of education. They're simply looking to get "some tail."

Don't even get me started on texting. Has dating, let alone, communication gotten so far gone that now it's acceptable to only speak through text. Not only that, text ALL day and then have the nerve to constantly ask for pictures? I'm not talking a nice head shot, these people are seriously asking for nudes. Seriously dude! Get a life. Please and thank you.

If they can't spare fifteen minutes of an actual conversation to offer intonation, inflection, volume, or pitch don't waste my time. They're either too busy to date, have no verbal communication skills or already in a relationship, in which case; you don't want them.

The sad thing is most of the people they're

dating accept it, so it becomes the norm and you're the social misfit for going against the standard and not accepting their behavior.   How rude! (Michelle Tanner voice)

      How about this incessant fixation of getting a picture of you sent to their phone. Once you say no, it's like you stalled and told them you'd send it in a minute, because that's all they ask about. No, no, and no, I will not send you a "pic" of me working, getting dressed, or lying in the bed. What the hell? Turn to Skinamax.

      Okay and what about this growing population of "whine and diners"? Where did they come from? Maybe you haven't experienced them, however; I can't imagine you haven't. They are the ones that offer you the world, including, but not limited to diamonds, pearls, and trips to the moon, purses, and shoes. Why? Don't get me wrong, I love a gift, and I do mean gift. Not collateral!! But some of you, yes I said you, are doing way too much after you get that little old outfit. It's bad for business, er, I mean bad for everybody else. Calm the hell down, and stop giving your best tricks up for a pair of Bakers shoes LOL! Okay, I attempted to be funny, but you get the point.

      Who, also, is this wonderful new breed of women paying men to be with them? Who raised you? Yes, I'm talking to you if the shoe fits. Why are you footing grown men's bills? They're not your brother, father, grandfather, son, cousin, hell; they're not even your man and you've gone broke giving this man money only for him to leave you for the woman he really wants.

      In the words of Tamar Braxton and now, Khrystian Nichole, "Get your life" and get it right. I've said before that dating is supposed to be fun, exciting, enjoyable and exhilarating. You're supposed to come from it either wanting to move forward or knowing to move on and keep a homie at the very least, but some of you just ain't doing it right.

Single Girl Gem #86

So many times you may find yourself out with a Lame, or just someone that you find yourself disinterested in and it almost always happens during the date. Couldn't be before, right? That's too much like right.

You may have begun the night with great expectancy, but let's face it; sometimes a guy will say something, do something or just plain old turn you all the way off. A way to politely "rid" yourself of their petty advances →

Guy: When's the last time you were held (insert any inappropriate verb here)?

Doll: Last night

Trips them up every time and they don't know what to say next. They had no business speaking to you in that manner. Of course you probably weren't even with someone the night before but if you're disinterested in the said person, and they say something disengaging; that's a great comeback or response to end the night sooner than later.

You're very welcome.

NOT up on the Popular Sex Culture Lingo

Excuse me, so when did the terms laid-up, kickin' it, or chillin' become the equivalent to what my old Pastor used to say, shackin' and smackin'? I don't know if that's just a way for someone to talk under your clothes, meaning: see where you are sexually or if the vernacular truly has changed amongst the masses and those statements are actually code for, "Don't bother me, I'm getting booty" or "I'm with a significant other-type."

However, here's what these following terms mean to me:

Laid-up→ Laying on the bed, couch or floor, usually significantly over the eight hour requirement for a good night's rest preferably in pajamas or some other alternative that you wouldn't ordinarily leave out of the house in. Occasionally family members or someone rather close to you could be present but don't play an active role in the equation. All forms of communication are applicable, except, coming over without warning because what you know of my beauty will be eluded by a bare-face, more than likely ashy skin, hair tied or all over my head, etc. However, if you don't hear from the person laid-up they've more than likely dosed off.

Kicking' it→ Enjoying oneself whether alone or with a large group, laughter is usually heavily involved, sometimes music is included. Text messaging is the preferred communication because otherwise I can't hear my phone and checking it or watching the screen is unacceptable.

Chillin'→ Primarily solo, but could also be with up to three others. It's very low key or more subtle. You can more than likely hold an applicable phone conversation.

Now, that I've lined them out no one should be confused about what I mean and there's no intricate code to break. Certainly no knuckle-headed "boy" should be questioning my interpretation any further.

Pervert or Sugar?

Is age really just a number? Can you truly embrace and relate to someone decades apart in age from you on a romantic level? Will you have regrets further down after being apart of a relationship where age is, in fact, a factor?

In this dating game, especially after a legal age of twenty-one, you are likely to meet someone a little bit older or younger than you, or possibly a whole lot older or younger than you. When you're the older of the two and your mate is half your age, you could be looked at as a pervert for basically dating a "child". Some may even look at you as if you're taking advantage of the younger person because of your experience and age.

When you're the younger of the two and your mate is half your age, you could be looked at as being manipulated or taking advantage of, but in some instances you're praised for making a come-up. Possibly gaining a "sugar-momma" or "sugar-daddy" because of the apparent age difference, and assumed increased income bracket that should be present.

I had a friend whom dated an obvious older man. They dated for the better parts of her life. Now, ten-plus years after she's been with him; she feels robed of her youth. He was older, so his ideals of fun, entertainment, and excitement were much different than hers. Because he was older, the more financial provider, and clearly the more experienced in life; she looked to him for advice, assistance, and leverage which now, ultimately she feels costs her years of her life.

Same situation with a guy I knew that dated an older woman. She was financially stable, had her own place, was "grown" and took care of him. Let's face it; for a twenty-two or twenty-three year older, that's a come up. He enjoyed their life together; that is, until he didn't. By the age of twenty-five he felt trapped and miserable. He wanted out.

I had another friend that dated a much, much younger girl. Yes, she was of legal age, and even had kids, but her circumstances and mind were immature. He enjoyed the "look" of having a younger woman on his shoulder but after awhile her immaturity weighed on him and he wanted out.

A lady I knew dated a younger guy. She enjoyed the "Cougar" title at first but after awhile she felt like a nagging mother asking him to pick up behind himself, taking care of him, etcetera, etcetera, and etcetera. I'm not saying this is the case all the time, or with each situation, but, I wonder...

Is age really just a number? Can you truly embrace and relate to someone decades apart in age from you on a romantic level? Will you have regrets further down after being apart of a relationship where age is in fact a factor?

Never-Ending Saga

Life is such a gift. You haven't the time or the energy to focus on negativity, animosity, dissension, excuses or games. Someone once said, "Water in the oceans can't sink a ship full of cargo, unless that same water fills it; likewise, negativity cannot take over your life unless you accept and take it in." Choose not to do it.

Some people are commonly the very people that boast positivity, maturity and righteousness; seem to cause their own negativity and then frustratingly blame everyone else. They ultimately are the problem, as well as, the solution but are so busy living in deception, fooling no one but themselves I might add; they con themselves into believing they're above any and all pettiness. Why would they do that though?

Why do some people feel the need to antagonize each other? Insult each other? Ultimately, ruin each other's day. It is a fact that there are just some people that no matter what; they start off on the wrong foot, don't get along, and or don't see eye to eye...ever. They don't mesh well. So the question remains! Why?

If you get so annoyed by someone's presence, why continue to go around them? If you don't like what someone says, why continue to ask them questions that require a response? If you don't like the way someone acts, why invite them around?

If you don't like the way someone salutes you, why continue speaking to them? If you don't like the service, why continue to patronize the establishment? If you don't like the gifts you receive, why continue exchanging?

I could go on big the fact question remains. Why? Stop setting yourself up for failure. Ultimately, whether you admit it or not, you're just hurting yourself, whether it is your feelings, or ego, or just plain old dignity. Stop doing things you don't like is my point. It's not worth it in the end or perhaps it's just you. Imagine that?

It's strange, even weird, that these types of people continue on with this saga. Now follow me here: They do something wrong to you. You confront them to place it behind you. They deny, lie or manipulate. They then turn the confrontation around. You get frustrated with their manipulation. They're upset with you that you're frustrated. They apologize inadvertently. You accept, tired of frustration. You pray to forgive them truly. You move on.

The cycle starts over. It's a NEVER-ending saga. That is, unless, you cut them out of your life cold turkey. However, since life is a gift, not to be thrown out like yesterday's garbage, you're not evil to them. Trouble with that is they adamantly continue to regain your friendship and trust through that window you leave cracked.

You, trying to remember Christianity, accept their apologies and attempt to move forward with them...they do something wrong to you....A NEVER-ENDING saga. The truth is people will be people. We are strange fruit.

Queers Chain

Accents, Smack scents. Depending on where you live or where you're from, everyone has an accent. Everyone, including me, always thinks it'll be romantic, sweet, sexy or all of the above to date someone with a distinct accent. Well I'm here to tell you that I was wrong.

So very wrong in fact, I couldn't have been more wrong. It's annoying, confusing and most of all frustrating. Annoying because I hated to hear my own name pronounced wrong and when it was close to correct; it sounded like a strained weasel....Queers Chain! Say it aloud and that's how my name was said.

He always began a sentence with my name too. I think he loved my name, or at least saying it but I hated it immensely. "Shut up already," I wanted to scream. If you know me, you already know I'd expressed my frustration, in a calmer more sedated version than screaming shut up of course! "Whuds I'm during Queers Chain?" Oh for the love of all things Vera Wang shut up, please.

No amount of handsome could cure the massive headache I'd suffer after a conversation with him either. What should have been quick, concise conversations all ended up turning into a tug-of-war of "huh", "what", "say that again", "repeat that one more time", "wait, slow down", and "one more time"! It was exhausting to say the least. At the end of a three minute conversation I was exhausted and ready to call it a night.

"Just text it to me!" Sure, that's what I would have said if text messaging was as prevalent then as it is now. That's it! The timing was off. My patience is a

work in progress, my tolerance or I should say, frustration, got the best of us. Queers Chain had to say good-bye, adìos, au revoir, arrivederci, ciao...you get the picture. It was a great memory, but certainly not a relationship built to last. I couldn't understand him and now that I think about it, he probably couldn't understand me either. It doesn't matter now; Queers Chain definitely left the building.

Vicious Cycle

Why does a person feel the need to excerpt themselves into your life even after you've made if clear to leave well enough alone. They should be grateful someone is willing to be kind enough to be upfront and honest in saying they want nothing to do with you and nothing from you. "Thank you but no, I don't want a friendship with you." "It won't work between us for multiple reasons you already are well aware of" "I'd appreciate it if you just stop calling me." "Please stop calling me. Have a nice life."

    There are so many people that get strung along, misused and abused so if a person can openly express how they feel about you or the intentions they have for you: you should accept it and move on, right, especially if they're not insulting you. Yes, perhaps your ego is tarnished, but come on, get over it. They could've said it in a rude, disrespectful way and then we'd have an entire other beast on our hands!

    Why harry ass, as my grandmother says, them about this incessant need to speak with them? Why must you need closure for a friendship? Why begin to insult in an effort to evoke an exchange? Why bribe with idiotic gifts that will never come to fruition? I just don't get it.

You're damned if you do and damned if you don't. They make you out to be the "bad guy" regardless when all you're really trying to do is save time, effort and energy. If you continue a friendship with someone even though you know without a shadow of a doubt it's going down a dead-end street; you're leading them on and wrong.

On the other hand, if you let them know upfront that you're not interested in them and have no desire to start or continue a relationship with them you're wrong and a plethora of other things. What gives? Take a hint. If a person wants you in their life; they'll make some type of conscious effort. Don't you agree? I mean seriously, there's other fish in the sea! If they don't see you're a great person; it's their loss, right?

You're great for someone! Consider yourself better off. You shouldn't have to throw yourself at anyone. Right? Besides you too old for that! (as my good friend says)

"I guess you really don't want me in your life."
-Seriously! Don't text a person this idiotic statement especially after it's been expressed. If it hasn't been expressed how about you just disappear anyway!
"I guess your cousin was right about you."
-Goodbye! Get lost. Now you're fishing.
"I just wanted to say goodbye"
-Bye boo. Bye!
"I guess I'll remove your name and number from my phone"
-Well considering I never call you anyway. Ok. Moving right along!

"I really need to talk with you."
-Really? About what and for what? Sit down clown!
But low and behold even after never responding you get a call and text from the number again during a holiday.
-Thought you removed my number. Damn Gina!
Then calls and text come from unidentified numbers.
-Really? Oh, sure; I'll answer an unknown number that's calling AND texting me saying the exact same BS.

     Even if you decide to be "nice", you think to yourself; I wouldn't want anyone to do this to my brothers or cousins or ME, so you answer or respond. Trying to be "nice" but making sure to be clear there's no light at the end of the tunnel for them. It still gets misconstrued and the vicious cycle begins again because the very thing you stopped communicating with them in the first place for is the very thing they continue to do: Annoy you. Against your better judgement being "nice" doesn't pay. Then we wonder why people just can't take a hint?

You MAY Possibly Be Psycho If...

We all know, or...err (clears throat to possible said individuals) have our very own likely "iffy" behavior and/or qualities. I'm NOT here to judge, and frankly...if you're good with them, hey- do your thang! However, I'm going to give you a little taste of my running list of psychotic behaviors.

     Mind you, again; I am no professional on matters of psychosis or psychology. I do not claim to hold any degrees, licenses, or certifications that would claim me otherwise. The following are scenarios, examples, experiences, or trends from my own personal testaments to some "iffy" behavior witnessed.

This section is mostly an added comic relief and is solely meant to poke fun of some of the outlandish "scenes" that could possibly happen during dating. If it happens to apply to you: Get help! If it applies to someone you know: Get thee behind you! LOL! But <u>SERIOUSLY</u>! Anything pertaining to you or people you know is purely coincidental.

You may possibly be psycho IF~

~You are stalking a person...whether it is social media, their house, job, calling and hanging up, etc. being anywhere unknown and unannounced numerous times and for extended time periods is freakishly weird. Please STOP and get a life.

You may possibly be psycho IF~

~You lie so often and (you think) so well that even YOU begin to believe your lies. If you're not a fiction or fantasy writer...what's the point? I mean, sooner or later all your lies are going to come out and you'll just look like some type of misfit that can't be trusted and everything that you say or said will become null and void! So do us ALL a favor and be true to yourself. Word is Bond. If you don't have your word...you have NOTHING. Believe dat.

You may possibly be psycho IF~

~You have the personality of two different people and in one sentence you're smiling, laughing and joking and in the next sentence you're cursing, hearing things, and flipping over tables. Get to anger management ASAP. No one wants to be around you any longer. You're a downer and, I might add, a little schizoid.

You may possibly be psycho IF~

~ You continually have regrettable moments each time you wake up from a night of binge drinking by yourself or socially. You have no recollection of the evening's events and you're constantly embarrassed and/or outraged by your actions. Seek help please. There are only so many, "I'm sorry's" your friends and support system want to hear. Deal with the real issues at hand before taking a swig.

You may possibly be psycho IF~

~You're living a double life. What's the purpose of all the aliases? And why don't you ever stay in the same place for longer than three months? And why can't you be around people in the long enough to hold open conversations? And where is your family or friends? And why does your social security card read, Randi but your name is Kendel? And where are you from eight in the morning to five in the evening because you don't have a job, but you're still never available? And....OKAY! LOL! I'll stop. I was getting into them. Ummm, yea...you already guessed; that's pyscho!

You may possibly be psycho IF~

~You live vicariously through a friend or relative so much so that you have spastic lapses in judgment and you cross the line between fantasy and reality. It's what we all remember as "the single-white-female" syndrome. Eek! Snap out of it...you're not them, you don't have *their* life. Their life experiences, triumphs, conversations and sadly...even problems are not your own. No matter how often you hang out with them, or get to know their inner circle; at the end of the day you are still YOU and merely just a thorn in their side. It's not flattering. You must seek professional help or at

the very least; get your own identity.
You may possibly be psycho IF~

~More than one person has characterized you or your behavior as such...men lie, women lie...BUT numbers DON'T! Kind, sweet, cute, funny, silly, great...these are adjectives worth being tagged to. Ain't nothing cute, kind or sweet about being tagged PSYCHO! As soon as someone
calls *you* or *your* behavior psycho...SOMETHING...I'm not saying anything in particular...but SOMETHING ain't quite right with you. Self-check!

Hope I've enlightened some folks today. If any of the above was you or someone you know; please don't hesitate to get help or call someone. There are specific help lines for the solutions to your problems. They're also on social media. It's all smiles...but there is REAL help for proper solutions. Get the help you deserve.

Obsession versus Love

The dictionary defines an obsession as this: obsession ob·ses·sion (əb-sĕsh'ən, ŏb-) n.
1. Compulsive preoccupation with a scheme or an unwanted feeling or sentiment, which is frequently accompanied by symptoms of anxiety.
2. A compulsive, often unreasonable idea or emotion.

I wrote this blog then because many people, maybe even you, confuse "love" with obsession. At the time a young lady had inboxed me explaining some, what she thought were, real emotions she had been feeling about a man she had barely known at the time. She'd met him, fell in love, and was having serious trust and security issues with him all in the course of about two and a half weeks before she'd written me for advice.

She'd had a pattern of meeting men, falling in love in short periods of time and then becoming obsessed with them only to have the relationship not work out in the end. She would be so involved emotionally with them, that she would isolate herself from her friends and family to avoid the embarrassment of her actions.

I've seen her since then. She's happy and healthy, picking up the pieces of her life and taking great care of her daughter. She's since gotten married as well to another man different from the one she assumed to be her soul mate at the time she inquired my help. She fell in love with her now husband fairly quickly as well, but this is a part of her truth.

Maybe you've never been in love, or maybe you've been in past abusive relationships with family, friends, or a spouse that now you don't really know what love is supposed to feel like, or maybe you think you've found your soul mate and this particular relationship is heaven-sent. I don't know, even understand, or want to fathom the reason for said emotions and obsessions, but as always; I've done a little research and have come up with my very own answer to the difference between LOVE and OBSESSION. Follow along...

In a particular article I read it said that there are different phases of an obsessive relationship. Obsession is different than love and has specific behaviors associated with each phase. The stages I came up with are appeal, restlessness, critical and obsession. In the article, they relate the phases to a wheel, because it continually goes on and on like some sort of sick merry-go-round and I agree.

APPEAL STAGE:

I think the initial stage is appeal. The article uses attraction, which is a synonym for appeal, but I think appeal better describes an instant or immediate attraction to another person.

Here are the red flags…

• Rushing into a relationship regardless of background knowledge, compatibility, or the amount of time you've gotten to know the person and not caring of distinct personality difference, or your deal breakers.

RESTLESS STAGE:

The proverbial point of no return, it happens usually after a commitment has been made to engage in a relationship.

Here are the red flags...

• Accusations of infidelity on the part of a partner and an incessant amount if dictating whereabouts or accountability for out of routine or daily activities.

• Attempts to control situations and be constant contact via phone, email or in person especially when you are or have been apart.

OBSESSIVE STAGE:

Here is where it becomes unhealthy. It is at this stage that obsessive behaviors are overwhelming the relationship. The person being the object of obsession usually begins to want out of the relationship. This stage is when the obsessed begins to lose control.

Here are the red flags...

• More serious accusations of cheating, especially if

THEY are doing the cheating. Perhaps they may become violently angry at small things you do in conjunction with someone they feel you are "cheating" with.
- Double checking and re-checking everything you do or say in the hopes to catch you in a lie or cause you to stumble with words.
- Guilt trips by questioning commitment to the relationship with the goal of manipulating and receiving more attention. They will try and alter previously set plan if they are not included.

CRITICAL STAGE:

It represents the fall of the relationship, due to all the other obsessive behaviors. It usually is serious and causes the object of obsession to get out as quick as they can. Prayerfully, it's not life-threatening. For a variety of reasons in the article they say; this is considered the most dangerous phase.

Here are the red flags...
- Feeling of hopelessness, loss, anger, rage, vengefulness, a combination or alternating feelings of each.
- Attempts to get the relationship back and promises to change

Check yourself before you wreck yourself.

Love is healthy. Love can be consuming, however, it is a state of mental bliss and delight. Love shows concern and dedication. Love is kind and peaceful. Love is a verb, an action.

FED Up!

In dating, if someone tells you they're fed up with you...it's time to move around. Situations, circumstances, etcetera will never be the same and they can't go anywhere but downhill from that statement. Think about it; when you're fed up with a job or something, it ordinarily means you're at the point of getting rid of it. Ridding yourself of the trouble and disposing of it entirely from your life. So when we say we're fed up with someone that's usually the same path we're taking.
If I were to break down the word fed, I'd say-
F=Finished
E=Exhausted
D=Disgusted

No one should ever feel disposable, because the truth of the matter is; people aren't disposable. But when we speak of being fed up we're at a limit...a peak...not only should you move around, but the person you're fed up with should move around too.

Wake Up!

Waking up to fussing on the phone, holding a conversation of digs and jabs is not a way to start a day with your significant other, right? If you're digging and jabbing, sending subliminal messages...is that enjoying each other or even liking each other? It certainly couldn't be love, could it?

This is not the scene for you. How does a simple hello, good morning turn into this twisted tale? There must be some underlying issues right? Right! Get to the root and figure it out, or hang up the phone and try it again. This is not the scene for love birds. I'm just saying...

Why... Episode #37

Why is it that when a man and a woman or talking it's not viewed as talking, but everything else....mostly inappropriateness? Men and women **can** communicate effectively, you know, without acting upon a physical or emotional attraction. Maybe not in all cases or in all instances, however; it **is** possible.

You can encounter a scene involving two attractive and available people talking and walk up to them without assuming they are dating, or flirting, or hooking up. Perhaps they are discussing work, religion, politics, planning a meeting of the minds, or maybe they are getting acquainted on another professional level. Either way it doesn't have to be an inappropriate scene or encounter.

Dating...With Children

It's a tricky, quite complicated scene. I've dated men without kids and men with kids. A person with kids never quite understands...or better yet, I'll say, never quite empathizes with the person without kids. It can be controversial and cause aching toes. Of course, relationships are most complicated **with** kids!
Questions will arise:
Do you even like kids?
Can you handle someone else's kids?
What's the parental relationship like with the kids?
How old are the kids?

How many kids?
When is the appropriate time to meet/encounter kids?
How fresh was the past relationship that the kids came from?
These questions are just the few that are involved, but somehow, extremely crucial in making the decision to date someone with kids. For me, in a perfect world...Khrystian's World...every relationship I encountered or at least felt a connection to would *not* involve someone else's kids, however; over the age of about twenty-five it could really be compared to finding a needle in a very large haystack...a man without kids, that is.

      Don't let him be easy on the eyes, great build, nice height...you know? Attractive! Don't let him be successful or at the very least goal-oriented. Then they're more likely to
have **multiple** kids, *especially* when you hit the dirty thirties! I'm not saying there aren't any single, unattached, available, successful, ATTRACTIVE men out there with **no** kids, but what I am saying is, like me; over thirty they're the exception to the rule. The unicorn!

      Trust me; this is not a knock on those of us with kids, without kids, or the kids themselves. It's just fact. MY facts. MY reality. And we can agree to disagree, but I'm telling you the sweet tea. To be quite honest; the easiest relationship involving kids is, sorry to say this, but if and when the kids aren't from a "relationship". Meaning: kids were a by-product of solely having sexual intercourse. Then; either the man has a relationship or not, but the kids aren't majorly factored into relationships. That's neither a bonus nor preference; again, it's just FACT.

Take a situation where someone that has about four kids, all from "sexual encounters" or quite possibly relationships, but none ever ended up with a serious commitment or marriage. The problem being; they only recognize and acknowledge, publicly, one of the children although they all know of each other and actually have a sibling relationship with one another.

Being a sincere Daddy's Girl, myself; I couldn't and wouldn't handle that situation and eventually, a relationship is dismantled. Take another situation where the man has a kid or kids but they live out of state. Then, you take another situation where the man publicly has multiple kids, but only one from a marriage, an actual commitment, and we wonder how it works?

Kids are important to him, so protection of the kids is important. I agree. Protection from what you ask? I'd say, protection from in and out's. One day they're in a relationship and the next day they're out. I have a problem with those that introduce their kids to *every* person they meet. That's just me!

Kids are kids. If and when you're serious and close to that "next step" of being in a commitment or a union that's a good time for the kids to meet the significant other. Someone once said they would prefer their kids and significant other to meet straight up and right away. So if there's friction and the kids don't like the person they're dating; they know right away.

A custodial parent that has total and complete twenty-four hour care for the kid, in essence, the kid lives with then might say something like that. The child is possibly exposed to the date picking them up, or seeing when the parent leaves, or getting dropped off by the parent on the way out.

Unless you plan to play hide and seek or tag for the beginning part of your relationship, it's probably best that after several dates and some form of commitment you introduce the children and significant other. It doesn't have to be formal and no titles have to be disclosed, but some form of awareness should be displayed. Otherwise you can make for some pretty uncomfortable moments and awkward feelings.

Most men, not all, but **most** have visitation set-up so the kids don't necessarily live with them. They visit. Have weekends, days or nights, or even just moments. It's easier said than done, per se. You can have a serious relationship and never have a "need" to meet their kids. Me, and coming from someone without kids, but who's experienced a lot directly and indirectly; I feel sharing your new relationship immediately, no matter how emotional you feel about them, isn't the best way if you're not the custodial parent.

If you tend to bore quickly, yourself, with a person you meet or if you're a serial dater, what's the use of the meeting and greeting, getting emotionally (or not) attached to the "newest" person for the kid? It's a drag. I loathe the revolving door of meeting and getting attached to the family, mother, father, grandparents, and etcetera of the man that I'm dating, and I'm an adult, so I know it has to be loathsome for kids. It really depends, clearly, on what works best for you.

With that said. Kids should remain in the kid's place and an adult remains the adult. They are the parent and decision-maker for what is best for the child.

A parent decides the right time and place, but never should there ever be disregard to either parties feelings. Protection of your kids isn't disrespect of your relationship and protection of your relationship isn't disregard of your kids. There should be a definite balance.

Your kids are just that; your kids. They can't do, say or make you feel the way your significant other does. If it were true, you'd be dating your kids, right? Right! That's gross...and so is treating your kids like you're in a relationship with them.

In the same manner your significant other can't, won't and shouldn't take the place of your kids because...well...that would just be weird too! But above this; it really depends on the people, the kids, the relationship, the kids' parent that's not in the relationship, as well. No matter how disengaged the two parents are. By the way; that person can be something else. Especially IF they still want them or have feelings for them. Ugh! They can then be annoying. Don't even get me started in on the bitter, broken or bruised one. That person just doesn't want their ex-whatever to be happy since they didn't have their happily-ever-after. That situation right there...just put that scene on pause or go on and delete it real quick. Seriously!

Long Distance Love

I have a friend that's dating someone and haphazardly, he moved away, over three thousand miles to be exact. He moved away to pursue law school; a goal he said he got away from due to this thing we call life. For him, life includes; two baby mommas. The question and scene was: Can a long distance relationship work?

     The circumstances being that the relationship is "new" although they have known each other for awhile, and that she, the person that remains; views time spent together as of the essence. I told her, it's not like he's off in another state because he loves surf board weather. He's there for a purpose, a career; a life-changing purpose.

     That in my opinion, of and within itself, warrants patience, understanding, and the conviction to remain with each other, especially since he made known his goal at the start of them dating. He was a little "off" for spontaneously up and leaving, but he IS free from distractions in another state. However, the question remains: can this work?

     I asked my followers what they thought and for feedback. The consensus was split. Some believed the relationship could work, while others were adamant that there was no way it could work. What do you think happened?

     After about a month, it didn't work. She wanted more. He wanted them to remain distant but together. Six months later they are both still very much so single, still living in two different states and of course he's still in law school.

     He still text messages her to check on her and tell her he loves her. She says it comes at inopportune times, just when she's ready to close the book and move on, his chime comes through alerting her that she's still on his mind. She wants to move on, and is casually dating but no one is sparking her interest. If you ask me; this case is not closed. The jury is still deliberating.

Scene

<u>One Act Play:</u>
You've been dating for years and it is love...OR...something kind of like it. There are faults on both sides and on all areas of the spectrum and it is still love...OR...something kind of like it so you build upon your piles of rubbish. There are some, could be more, outside kids involved but there's love...OR...something kind of like it so you still marry. There have been breaks and pain but it is still love...OR... something kind of like it. Dramatically unveiled there's not just one, but the number two. Same time...Same way...Same... (Clears throat, gives a side-eye, and leaves it alone) in addition too. There's love...OR...something kind of like it. You choose to stay for love...OR...something kind of like it. A choice you make for love...Or...something kind of like it. Same choice is made to leave after time, some time, plenty of time, too much time. You're done. Where's the love...Or...something kind of like it?
End Scene.

"Up" Kind of Love

Isn't it funny that in the "moment" that you're in your relationship with someone you think; this is absolutely A.mazing! He/she is the one for me. I am in love! What the heezy was I ever doing with that (insert insult here) in the first place? I wasted so much time on that (insert another insult here) and all this time I could have been living this great life with (insert sickening

mushy name here).
    Sound familiar? Well whether that's your case or not; whether it happened in this relationship, or you realized it after the seven year crush you had on the guy that doesn't know you exist; it's happened to some, to most, to the best of us.

    A few months ago, I was having this conversation with a friend of mine about love and if we really believed in it. Now don't go getting your panties in a bunch. God is love. Yes we know that and we believe whole-heartedly in God's love for us and within us. It was just a simple conversation about relationships; the lack there of, and the common misconceptions of said relationships. So before you go bible thumping to me; let's keep it real, sane and remove all the holier than thou (oh no, not the preacher's kid) judgments for the purposes of this discussion.

~Now back to our regularly scheduled program~

    My friend and I both agreed in real love; but I then began to question if there was really such a thing as a true love. You know, the forever love? The kind that you read about, hear songs about, watch movies about; and even hear the old wives' tales about the man that only had one true love and when his young wife died an untimely death he never loved again (story of my great grand-father may he rest in peace).

    I just wonder. Because nowadays, you hear the stories and have the friends that fall in love at first sight and marry after three months. Then divorce after six months. You hear the stories and have the friends that date and love for eight years and then marry. Get divorced in three years. There are couples that were together for over twenty years, that watch as their children graduate college, embrace grandkids, and all of a sudden they don't love each other any longer and they split. But truly, that's all facts and figures, because nowadays you just can't tell.

People aren't made up of what they used to be made of. Men and women, alike, don't sugar coat or pussy-foot around issues like they did back in the day. There are no more of the: Don't ask. Don't tell policies. People aren't playing games with their hearts anymore. We're asking and we're telling even if you don't want to hear it. So I'll leave the marriage issue alone and just keep with the discussion of true love. Strength and length of marriage is a whole 'nother topic...in which at the time, I don't even have the strength to partake in.

Back to true love.

I just figure. You get into a relationship. You fall in love (and for some vice versa). You maintain a relationship. You believe it's the BEST relationship ever and you believe you've never felt a love like this one right now. Until, that is you do. Because...you break up! Whoa! Blind-sided! He's or she's not the person you like to have believed they were.

You start again. You get into a relationship. You fall in love (and for some vice versa...moving on). You maintain a relationship. You believe it's the BEST relationship ever and you believe you've never felt a love like this one right now. Until, that is you do, because...you break up. Damn. Not again. You thought you knew him or her so well this time.

You decide; I'm taking a break. I need time for myself. I fall hard and they just can't accept me for me. They don't deserve my love. That is until... You get into a relationship. You fall in love (and for some vice versa...whatever). You maintain a relationship. You believe it's the BEST relationship ever and you believe you've never felt a love like this one right now. That all the "crap" you put up with before all led you to this perfect relationship with this perfect person.

Until, that is, you do because...you break up! You thought he or she was perfect. Your families got along; you were really on the trail to marriage. You were looking at rings and all. That was your soul-mate. That was the end of the line for you. No one could compare.

Enough is enough you think. You've had enough heart breaks for one person to stand. Maybe you're destined to be a bachelor/bachelorette for life. There's nothing wrong with that, you think. Lots of people have a great life being single. You plan the perfect getaway with your friends. You need time to re-evaluate your life and what you'll do next.

It's time to get foot-loose and fancy-free in the city, and why not? You're young! You're single! You've got a great career and family and personality! It's about time to put it to use. That is until...You get into a relationship. You fall in love (and for some vice versa...enough already, you get it). You maintain a relationship. You believe it's the BEST relationship ever and you believe you've never felt a love like this one right now. Until, that is you do. Because...you break up!

Do you see my pattern of logic? Each time you are in a relationship; you figure that's the love of your life. Your soul-mate. The one God put on this planet specifically designed for you! Until, that is, you break up; and he's or she's NOT! I just simply believe that whomever you're in a relationship with at the time is your "true love"!

So there it is. Is there ever really a true love? Is there a difference between true and real love? How do you know? What happens if and when you're not in a relationship with your "true love" anymore? What will you say then? How do you truly know you're in love?

What? Is it that you miss them even before they leave, because you can miss a city or a homie like that? Is it because you get sick at the mere thought of losing them? Give me something really expensive and I don't necessarily mean monetarily and I bet I'll get real sick at the thought of losing it too! I mean, honestly.

Open Discussion

A group of people were holding a discussion once about finding someone you can look at and say, "He's definitely the one!" Now to be clear, you know my viewpoint on the definitive ONE. You only need one, but as it relates to love; they were discussing; how do some people actually realize when they've found "that one"?

They remarked it was the one you want to spend the rest of your life with and have four kids with. The one you don't mind going through this thing we called life with. Since I haven't personally experienced that sensation for myself, I didn't interject my opinion as it relates to how some people say they are certain the moment they find the one.

    If you don't know really know someone and you just met them, then you don't know if they have quirks that will bug you for all-time. You don't know background, beliefs, religion, origin or future destination, and you certainly don't know anything about them; at least for a year. There's some debate about my timeline, I know. But alas! I interjected.

    I called up another friend and our conversation started a bit like this. I asked a friend specifically about her and the flavor of the week she was dating. Mind you she's been dating him off-again and on-again for approximately three years. However, take my word for it; the off-again far outweighs the on-again. Any who! She said it was going fine and that she liked him (have to stop right here...because THIS is major)

    She ever, hardly ever says she actually likes someone. She may say, "He's cool, he aight, he'll do, he's really not my type," but she ever, hardly NEVER says she LIKES someone! So believe me; when she said this. I put down the phone...changed to speaker...perched carefully in my seat...all attention on her...and listened...intently.

    She went on to say; "He's seemingly an all-around great catch. He's shown he likes me, I've shown him; I like him. He's asked me a few underlying things in conversation about my future, and kind of where "our" future would lead based on what we've been talking about. I like him but, I just don't know if he's the one I'm supposed to be with and do I need to be more serious, or do I need to wait it out, because he just might not be the one, and I'll miss out on the actual one I'm really supposed to be with. You know?"

Now, some of you may have been down this same road my friend discussed before. Some of you have on your sour judgmental puss-face right now. Some of you are just shaking your head at me and my dear friend, and some of you may wish you could stop reading right now, get to jotting down a note and sending it to my email, khrystian08@hotmail.com and then find out who this friend is so you can give her your very own advice! Well I'm here to say, Stop it now.

Whatever it is good or bad, because what's good for the goose is great for the gander. Everyone has to go through their own life experiences and face their own truths.
My thing is this. She's MY friend, so I get to tell her. (Sticks tongue out) and I did.

No one is perfect. The grass is never greener on the other side. What you may dislike about one man, you will loathe with the next. This in NO WAY means to settle, EVER. It simple means, you have to be mature. It's also imperative that you know your breaking-point. Everybody has their breaking-point and their list of do's and don'ts no matter what you say.

The only thing for her to do, at this point, is to not waste more time, especially if she doesn't want him. Clearly, it's not meant to be if she has all those questions. She has to decide straight-up if she enjoys spending her time with him. Does his mere sight disgust her? Does he vex her? Do the two of them have any deal-breakers (For those that forgot 1. Religious differences 2. Moral differences 3. Extreme social differences 4. Economic differences)

Is he abusive? Does his good outweigh his bad? These are among the things to consider. Are any of the negative scenes in this chapter indicative of the relationship you have and if so, how are they addressed? If you're just not that in to him, then move on, and keep it stepping. But, if by chance you are into him, and there is something there; see what happens!

You can't live life with should've, could've would've (s) and you definitely can't live life waiting on the next best thing, you may wind up coming up short. You'll be by yourself and eventually watching him walk down the aisle with her and all you'll be able to do is cry. (Like my girl Etta James sings)

Have plenty of Happy "True" Love Moments or Scenes, as I like to call them.

It's Me, Not You

I've come to the definitive conclusion; based solely on my life experiences, and with all that continues to come my way that it's me and not anyone else that's responsible for the life I live. The life I accept, rather. From my business career choices to my personal relationship choices.
I used to live in denial. I used to act dense. But now, today, for sure; I know it's me!
No one else!
Me!
I'm choosing the people I meet, befriend, date, fall for...I'm choosing the bad decisions, mishaps, disasters...I'm choosing the heartaches, heartbreaks, headaches...
It's my fault! It's my bad. I'm in the wrong.
I've been annoyed, offended, and irritated by everyone but the one person that's responsible and that's me!
I've been blinded. Thinking I was innocent in single-handedly ruining, damaging, and destroying my life. I, indeed, have been the culprit!
Why though?
Perhaps it was because I was naive. Maybe it was simpler to blame everyone else. Could it have been vulnerability? Or, dare I say, weakness. No! Couldn't be that, right?! Not weakness? No one ever wants to truly admit their weaknesses, right?
I've lied to myself. I've manipulated myself. I've had a hidden agenda with my damn self!
The first step to recovery is admittance right? The first stage in releasing demons is to expose them, right...and they flee?
So here it is:
It's ME, not you!

Chapter 11
New Relationship Rules

You know, life is a funny thing. Who would have ever imagined me giving relationship rules? The Queen of Singledom! Yes, yes, I know. All of you that know me personally are most definitely reading this thinking...*my how times have changed.* It's amazing where life can bring a person.

Us single girls don't stay single always. When we're single, we master the art of our singledom, and we gather all our gems. We date, have fun, live life, travel, experience new things, enjoy ourselves, and apply all of life's lessons that come our way.

Sooner than later we attach ourselves to someone we actually like spending our time with. After a few frogs we may stumble upon a prince. We discover our deal breakers; we play our roles in various scenes and a few episodes. We haphazardly endure awkward moments, there are some bad dates and some good dates, and we have a few rants but we definitely grow in love.

It doesn't stop there. Once you get into a relationship, no matter the amount of commitment you've made the gems sparkle brighter and new rules begin to apply. A whole new set of rules within the relationship where it's not all about you anymore it, now, involves someone else. That someone else is someone you adore and care about or you wouldn't have made the commitment to begin with.

I have come up with a few "rules" of relationships that I think are simplistic enough to follow and with the right combo can be quite satisfying. These rules are for the fresh and new relationship, but most of the premises are also totally applicable for the seasoned relationship as well.

New Relationship Rule 1

Timing is everything and in more ways than one.

1. When dealing with hectic daily schedules, like work, it could seem difficult to make time to spend together. Cut that issue off at the head. Make the time! It'll take extra effort at first, and some compromising on the logistics (where, when, for how long, etcetera.) but once it's established; you're back smooth sailing.

2. Response time is critical. When replying, confirming or denying. How do you respond to conflict? How you handle or, not handle, praise? How often do you accept or reject new and different ideas? It's all relevant. It all matters and it all can add value or devalue your new relationship.

Those are just a couple of things to think about as you begin and maintain your new relationship. Make time for each other both physically, by seeing each other and emotionally, by genuinely set aside time to concern yourself with how your significant other thinks or feels about situations, no matter how small. Consciously map out time for each other even if it's a short, simple, and sweet, *"Thinking of u"* text.

Always think about those little ripples that can eventually make a BIG splash, especially if you allow it, and this can be positive or negative. At the very least, start off in the positive and use your time wisely. Have fun learning each other.

New Relationship Rule 2

You and your Significant Other should enjoy each other. Spending time together, getting to know each other. If, when you make plans together, you feel like you're doing a chore, move around because that's not a good sign. Time won't make it any better; it'll just exhaust you before the end.

New Relationship Rule 3

If you enjoy each other's company, spend time together. Spend time together without concerning yourself with outside voices, opinions, or interference. Not everyone has great chemistry with their mate, so if you're fortunate enough to enjoy each other's company doing absolutely nothing. Ride that mofo to the wheels fall off. That just simply means...ENJOY your moment.

New Relationship Rule 4

Everybody has a past, that's what makes us who we are. Each relationship you enter into, in a perfect world, should begin with a clean slate and NO misconceptions or lingering skeletons. Unfortunately, however; that's not always the case. Know when to be candidly open and when minor details and trivial nuances can be laid to rest.
Word to the wise; if it will affect your current relationship: DISCLOSE
If it will NOT affect your current relationship: leave well enough alone
Here are two very specific examples of when to DISCLOSE and when to leave alone:
1. I was kicked out of student council in 7th grade for

getting into a fight at the school dance. (Leave alone)
2. I currently have a restraining order on me for a bar fight I had a few months before I met you.
(DISCLOSE)
See the difference?

New Relationship Rules 5-13

NRR 5 Be with someone that celebrates you not tolerates you. It's hard out here enough as it is. You want to be with some one that doesn't wear you down, but builds you up.
NRR 6 Know what you want. The first step to getting what you want is having the courage to get rid of what you don't want.
NRR 7 If someone screws up let it go. If they keep screwing up, let them go. It ain't worth all that.
NRR 8 Being intimate is NOT just a physical act. Make emotional, spiritual and mental connections as well.
NRR 9 See the BEST in your significant other and help them do the same.
NRR 10 Sulfuric acid for love is fighting below the belt, i.e. name calling or finger pointing. Do not do it.
NRR 11 Behave badly together...harmless guilty pleasures people. Nothing you could go to jail for!
NRR 12 Keep the element of SURPRISE alive.
NRR 13 Get rid of EXtosterone! Yes I made up the word. I love it. It means let go of the ex's. They are not to be included in your new relationship. You're not together for a reason.

NEVER really single!

Okay ladies and gentlemen, this is a good place to stop and discuss a post I wrote that most definitely applies to that last new relationship rule concerning EXtosterone. EXtosterone is important and, if you allow it, can cause several problems within your new relationships. Either because you like to have your cake and eat it to, or you don't have the guts to truly break loose of a relationship that's no good for you.

EXtosterone is the produced by the ex-relationship you had and it is the act of still maintaining a relationship that causes dissension to your new relationship. Or otherwise keeps you from sincerely moving on.

Let's face it, once you get past your latter twenties; you're never really single. You may not be in a monogamous relationship, but when you first meet someone, you proclaim, "I'm single!" You're NOT! There are loose-ends, off again-on again relationships, honey dips, cutty buddies, booty calls, "friends" with benefits, and we can't forget the oh-so-popular PROVERBIAL rebound! Call them any name you want, other than "significant other", but trust me; you have them. And I say them, because for some of us; there are more than just one!

This person, to whom you are actually involved with, no matter how infrequent, is the person(s) that you ignore the moment you call yourself trying to assume a new relationship with someone else. They are the person, more than likely, that doesn't know about your infatuation with the new "boo". They are usually last to find out, especially when it comes to just how serious you are with the new "boo". Heck, sometimes they don't find out until the social media photo album of your nuptials. EGAD!

You may engage the loose-end or elude to the fact that you've taken an interest in someone other than them, and by elude, I mean through ignoring calls, not-so available behavior, irritability, any bizarre changed behaviors, inadequacies in bed, or just totally not into them in bed, etcetera. However, you still continue to dangle the bait by calling every now and again, sending a nude picture, sending a "lovely" email or text informing them of how much you love, admire, respect and miss them, evasiveness, omission of details, treating them to brunch, drinks, etcetera, because let's face it; you don't know how far you'll actually get with your new "boo".

They may turn out to be so totally not the one, and rather than risk being, dare I say it; ALONE, you string your loose-end along for the ride, also can be known as EXtosterone based on the significance of the loose-end. Is this fair? I think not, but is it realistic...most definitely.

Here is an example:

Without Me

Based on a text conversation encountered....The first verse and chorus of a song titled, Without Me, couldn't have said it any better for me than if I simply snap shot the text and aired all the dirty laundry myself. My ex-boyfriend was officially out of line and for no good reason. Listen; if you have a new chick professing her love for you, and you're showcasing your "love" so hard on social media sites by posting something as idiotic as watching television to prove how "happy" and "in love" you are every other day, then please move around and be more than happy. Everyone gets it....you pay your cable bill, as my lovely line-sister said. Stop communicating with your ex-girlfriend that, *I'm dating but I'm not married, engaged nor do I have a girlfriend where I'm in an exclusive relationship*

Or

I will always love you more than anything or anyone

Or

She knows about you and that I'm not ready to have anything serious with her based on the way I feel about you

It's NOT cool at all to any party involved. If I had a new "man" that I was expressing my undying gratitude that he entered my life and loved me unconditionally, I certainly wouldn't want him expressing those truths, facts, and especially lies to his ex-girlfriend in any form or fashion. So...I say all that to say, leave EXtosterone alone. It doesn't belong in a new relationship.

    A great catch, sure they're out there, they may even be "single", but I'm sure behind EVERY "single", "available", "great catch" there is a loose-end that needs to be tied up, cut, and dead-bolted please, at least before you indulge into a fresh and new relationship. Take it from me; tested, tried and true, it tremendously saves on confusion, awkwardness, hurt feelings, long-term issues and the inevitable break-up.

Good dating is so enjoyable, fun, motivating, and all that other good stuff, and no, please do not tell each person you date about the other person/people you date. That's just plain old goofy. You date as many as often as you like. There's nothing wrong with dinner and a movie. However, when you change the game and make it into a monogamous relationship, your loose-ends need to be cut off. N.

Single? Be single...the test to see if you're REALLY single or not; is if you don't have ANY explanations to give to NOT one person! But guess what? After the latter parts of your twenties you're NEVER really single...unless of course you live in cave and haven't ever had any type of relationship in your life! Go figure! Happy Not Really "Single"

New Relationship Rule 14

Once, and if, you've found yourself in a relationship, fresh and new or old and established; it's important to remember to handle with care! If your mate hurts your feelings by something they've said or an action they've shown; it's important to openly express the way they made you feel exclusively with them instead of retaliating with a negative snow ball effect!
In a relationship, two people are intended to generally care for each others' feelings.

My advice is to not be so quick to jump to the defensives. Acknowledge that if you've chosen to be in a relationship with them, you've also chosen to trust them with your heart, and although there's no guarantee you won't get hurt or heart-broken, believe that if you express your feelings in a mature, sensitive, and proactive manner; all things will work out just fine and they will apologize, or at the least acknowledge your feelings.

Chapter 12
Open Letters to the Guys

Hello Gentlemen!

I have gotten an overwhelming amount of support from you about my blog posts. Some of you have personally reached out and thanked me for the posts, a few of you have made post suggestions, and many of you have commented on the posts, and most importantly you've indicated that you read and look forward to my posts.

It means so much to have a broader audience than just the single girl, or solely women, because everyone one can benefit from gems given in life and you've certainly broadened my topics and given me depth of perspective in my writing about the single girl, for the single girl, with the single girl in mind. I have to say thank you from the bottom of my heart for that.

I have just a few things to say to you all. This letter isn't specific to one man or a certain type of man and it is certainly not to say that this letter is meant for all of you. Just like the single girl, you are unique and different and no one person is the same. If it doesn't apply to you great, but if it does…self check!

At this time, I'm mostly addressing the way some of you approach, come at, and respond to the opposite sex! I don't know who is writing the "new book" but you need to take it, burn it, and whoop the guys' ass that wrote it!

Using a different adjective and pronoun with every sentence you say to females' borders on gross. Most times a simple, single "Good morning" will do. Please lose the; "Good morning sexy lady", Good evening pretty dove," I could go on, but it turns my stomach (Yuck!) This especially rings true when it's not your woman. That's different; you and she may have that type of relationship with one another. I'm talking about random women you encounter and you have the audacity to double adjective/pronoun her!

Continue chivalry, please. It's not dead! Yes, I realize there are these "new breed independent" women in the world that can make it difficult. But, I must say; you will lose your "man-hood" calling card each time. Take for instance you stop doing the supposed "man-things" in the relationship and stop being a leader; you'll have a serious problem when your "man-hood" is checked, questioned or demeaned. Try not to set yourself up for failure. Discuss roles and the lane each of you will stay in. It saves time, embarrassment and uncomfortable situations!

Stop handing out these business cards. If you're about business...be about it business and stop mixing it with pleasure. Unless the lady asks for your card; she just may not use it. Again, setting you up for failure. If she's like me; she'll either place the card on the table, not even looking at it, or she'll give it back to you and tell you to put it away.

Just because someone makes eye contact with you; it does NOT automatically mean she's interested in you! Enough said and please don't get offended and abusive with your tone and language when the lady decides she doesn't want to exchange numbers, take you up on your offer to buy her drink or dance. She's not mean or stuck up, she's unavailable.

Umm...also, some conversations are intimate, personal and are better left for when you know the lady a little bit better! If you didn't meet her in THAT particular type of setting, where anything goes; it's NOT appropriate! Err...I'll just leave it at that. I'm sure you can use your imagination.

Be Deliberate and crystal CLEAR about your intentions. I believe it's called, "keeping it one hundred", per my dear guy friend. Remember that toys are for kids, so NO woman deserves to be "toyed" with. And, as I most often times tell my single eligible bachelor friends; "More often than not a woman wants the EXACT same thing you want." Just be upfront and if she can deal with your bottom line; she ain't going nowhere

Honesty is Sexy! And heck, if she can't handle it...you don't want her anyway. You need someone strong and deliberate just like you.

Random Rant

I don't understand why men's actions don't mirror what comes out of their mouth. Okay, okay, it's not just men, but you're who I'm addressing right now.

Why tell a woman you love her, or want to spend your life with her or there's no one else you want to be with. If what you say, couldn't be further from the truth. I read a quote that said, "Your actions speak so loudly, I can barely hear what you're saying." It's truth. Men will say these things and have a relationship with a woman, but have another woman, some side chick, thinking their unhappy in a current relationship. That it's just a situation they're in and not able to get out of quite yet.

Women will eat it up too. Feeling dominant over the supposed girlfriend or wife, who is what she thinks, naive to the fact that her so-called man, doesn't want her. Please believe a woman, or anyone for that matter, usually won't stay in a relationship where they are feeling truly mistreated or neglected. So trust and believe that you, Sir, are undoubtedly not telling her something or better yet, you're doing something to make her stay.

Some men will literally live a double-life. Pretending to not have a charge on their phone, or lose their phone, or be asleep in an attempt to not speak to one of the women, be working late, or too tired to be intimate with a woman. A man will act stressed out financially so he doesn't have to wine and dine a woman. He will even go so far as to take off from his job to make time for his side-chick. All true stories and situations.

Why do men feel the need to lie and manipulate a situation instead of being open and honest with the assumed woman they love? Most times a woman wants exactly what you want, especially in these liberal days of dating. A woman will act as the stereotypical man and she will sleep with you and have no strings attached, so men, you don't actually have to play mind games.

Then there are some people that are so selfish, or immature, or just plain old ignorant that they don't understand the concept of loyalty, love and dedication. Love is not, as Halle Berry said in the film Boomerang, "some disease you catch like the plague", it's an emotion that no one is personally asking of you.

Of course relationships are cool, but playing the field is great too, especially when you are not ready to settle down. I get it. However, if you are inappropriately talking to someone other than your intended significant other, for instance, asking sexual favors, sending nude pictures back and forth, meeting up with them privately, or not able to be around them in the presence of your actual significant other. Then you're not living right and you need to move around from the relationship because you're obviously not ready to settle down.

You're not being fair to the person you're lying to. You're selfish and deceitful, hurtful and ruining a life that someone is possibly trying to commit to. I get that you don't understand the magnitude of what you're doing when you date around or don't accurately communicate your intentions but it's actually a serious matter.

You should go on your merry way. Don't commit if you're not ready and don't feel pressured to commit when you're not ready. Indulge in those women that caused you to do so much damage in the first place; don't make yourself look like the bad guy any longer with innocent, unsuspecting women.

Hypocrisy Brewing

A pot is being stirred. It's a big ol' pot too and it's filled to the brim with hypocrisy, coupled with a side of double standard. I get it too. We live in a society of "do as I say and not as I do". Too bad that hasn't been working out too well. I'm here to say; what's good for the Gander is great for the Goose. If you didn't know, now you do.

You cannot, I repeat not, expect someone to live according to the rules of said-individual terms and you not hold yourself to the same standard. Who thinks like that? A hypocrite that is who. Why do people feel the need to place others to a higher standard than themselves? They, for a lack of better words; place others on pedestals hoping, wanting and actually believing they can keep that pedestal locked up behind a glass protective shield for later use; for their mere enjoyment and entertainment.

The hypocrite places these ridiculous stipulations on someone that they most definitely aren't living up to, and when they figure out that the jig is up and others can "play the game" just as good, if not, even better; then and only then, do they get their little feelings hurt. Things and situations don't revolve around anyone in their own "little" world. The sooner you get an understanding of that, the better off you'll be. Err, I mean the hypocrite.

How about this notion? Treat others the way you desire to be treated. Don't do to someone what you wouldn't want done to you. Be a person of your word. If you say it or feel it, mean it. Don't play games. Think of the consequences of your actions first. Life would be so much sweeter. Imagine that.

Best Regards,

Khrystian Nichole

Chapter 13
Life Gems

A Hard Act to Follow

Beautiful is one of those acts that are hard to follow ...and keep up. If you allow it; it can be a ton of pressure to maintain, it comes with a price. Let's face it- everything does, even your life; Jesus did pay it all, and it takes much work to live up to. The one great thing is: Beauty is in the eye of the beholder!
When you find those that coin you beautiful, those that believe you're beautiful, the ones that greatly value your beauty: Treasure them.
The treasure isn't that they're using the adjective beautiful flippantly or providing you with a compliment... The real golden nugget is that you are your natural self, flaws and all, without additives being Beautiful!
Toast to Us,

Beautiful Ones that know how to Work It!

Our Greatest Hater

I'll tell you the honest to goodness truth and this will change your way of thinking if you clasp hold to it. What I'm about to reveal will save you from heartache, confusion, discomfort, delusion and pain...
Time is your greatest hater!

      Honey, time will wear your ass out. Time will put you in your place when you act like you forget. Time will have you fatigued and lethargic. It will most, without doubt, run circles around you. Time will remind you where you have been and just where you are headed.

      Act like you don't know that fact if you want to. Get out there and attempt to do the things you did twenty or even ten years ago and see what happens. Watch and see how Time molly-whoops your ass straight. You will wake up bruised and confused. Go on and try Time. It is not playing with you.

      Time won't wait on you to figure it out either, and it does not care how long it takes you to catch on because unlike everything we have and know...it's infinite. It is ferocious! Time is unapologetic!

      You can't beat Time if you had a stick. No matter how much of it you spend, how long you spend it, and to what degree you spend it; sooner or later, Time will prove your efforts were all a waste.

      I could continue to go on and on about Time and just how much it hates us all. It does not in any way discriminate. Time hates on us all equally, and without fail. Some of us handle Time differently. Some of us handle time with care and it shows. Time may be more generous with some than others, but we are all caught in Time's wrath. Do not bother with your complaints about all the other so-called "haters" Time is indeed the unrivaled hater you have.

Forgiveness and Mistakes

"Nobody can go back and start a new beginning, but anyone can start today and make a new ending." - Maria Robinson

Asking for forgiveness means: I won't need this pardon again. It does not provide a temporary solution. Forgiveness is long-standing and is honored only if offered in the same manner. Stop making the same mistake twice because after the first time it is a CHOICE. Commit to your pardon. Stay loyal to the forgiver.

Likewise, forgiver; have confidence that you can forgive them whole-heartedly without cause for retribution. I understand it sometimes can be hard. When you've been lied to so much it becomes hard to believe the truth and that is where a problem lies. When asking for forgiveness, be sincere, humble and faithful in your words. Choose the words wisely and do not make empty promises. Your word is your bond.

Most times all you would like is for the person that wronged you to ACKNOWLEDGE that they have hurt or upset you. You cannot control other people and their actions or reactions so there is no need to ask for acknowledgment, an apology or even a change, but life would be so much smoother if everyone regarded each other in the same regard, they themselves would expect to be regarded and cared for.

The dictionary defines acknowledgement as a noun in five assortments of form:

n.
1. The act of admitting or owning to something.
2. Recognition of another's existence, validity, authority, or right.
3. An answer or response in return for something done.
4. An expression of thanks or a token of appreciation.
5. A formal declaration made to authoritative witnesses to ensure legal validity.

  In most cases all it takes is recognizing someone's hurt, pain or feelings. Even if you are hell-bent on thinking or knowing you have done absolutely nothing wrong, you cannot control how you make another person FEEL. Simply acknowledge their feelings and move on. There is no omission of guilt or blame, you are merely acknowledging.

  Now; there are some people that hold grudges and harbor resentment forever no matter what you say or do and that is their headache in the overall scheme of things. At least you have done your part in acknowledging how you may have made them feel and explained your intent. Therefore, you can sleep well at night and the other person can begin their healing process once they let it go.

Age Ain't Nothing but a Number

I hear this more often than I care to share and it is typically from insecure, insufficient people but that is just my opinion. These people always seem to have a judgment about the appropriate or inappropriate characteristics of a person in distinct age groups.

Could someone tell me who has read an age-informational dictionary that displays when you look up the number eight-teen all the characteristics, activities and thoughts of an eight-teen year old? Who in their right mind created this same age-informational dictionary that specifies in great detail the particular way of life for a forty year old? Do you see how ridiculous beyond doubt this is?

Oh I know; it must be the same people that tell you what major life change you should have at particular ages. You know; the one that makes you feel horrible for not having a child at twenty or for not being married by the time you graduate college or them that shun you for deciding to go back to school or open that business to finally follow your dreams. Yes; we are speaking of them.

Please, if you are guilty of doing this, STOP, at once. It is exasperating and you ought to not be placing stipulations on how you or anyone else lives life. No one should be allowed to do that to anyone for that matter. Placing fences around or glass ceilings up are not components of great success stories. In the moment you do that, you stop living and achieving.

I can give you a good example of what I mean. I have a friend that met, fell in love with a much, much older mate, and got married. By much, much older; I simply mean the mate was older in mind, and age, and experience. The mate had been there, done that with many things my friend hadn't even begun to experience because my friend was straight out of high school from a small town and had not seen or experienced much just to be quite honest.

The mate would always say, "We don't do that

anymore, that is too child-like" or "No, we will not be doing that because it is silly and child-like." My friend would agree, even the activities were designed with her personality, and age-group in mind. I am in no way blaming the mate at all for the missed opportunities or activities my friend did not partake in; I'm simply stating facts that occurred in their relationship. My friend most positively made her own personal decisions.

Long story short, they are not married any longer. That is no big surprise seeing as how their incompatibility increased as the years went on. At this time, my friend wants to experience the same things the mate disapproved of then. The very activities he deflected her from then, she quite naturally wants to engage in.

She allowed, thorough her own admission someone to deter her from the things she desired to do and now, she feels as if she missed out on the better parts of her life. She now admits that she wishes she would have experienced them at the same time those she grew up with did, because now the things she desires to do everyone else has a, "been there, done that attitude" and no longer want to participate.
That's just one scenario...

Another friend of mine thinks it is too immature to refer to women as girls. She says she's a woman, so on invites for "Girl's Night", a phrase of endearment, she takes offense to the verbiage. Girl, in case you are like her and do not know, is the shortened form of the slang term girlfriend, indicating a female sister-friend to another female.

It does not imply that someone is excusing the fact that you are an adult. It's a ding dang on word. A slang term, that is common and used as a term of endearment. No one says, "Woman's Night" because to be quite frank; it doesn't roll off the tongue as smooth. It is boring. Ladies Night, yes this is another way to address a sister-friend, but to be clear; it does not make you any less an adult for saying girl.

The point is to live your life and love it. If, at sixty, you want to go to Disney world get a ticket and go. If you have the means and ability live your life. Why does there have to be an age stipulation on something or someone? When someone opens their mouth and abruptly says to me something I'm too old to be doing, I do it anyway and when it is accomplished, dare them to continue placing stipulations on me.

Do BETTER

When you know better, you should do better. When you do better, you will receive better which is the best news. For instance, if you know you are not living up to your potential, what are you waiting on? How will you ever know when that glass ceiling has been removed, if you won't even jump high enough to touch it?

Remember what you are worth and stop settling. Once you know you are greater than what you have been accepting from others whether it is on your job, in the church choir, or in a relationship; you will stop settling for someone or something that is incapable of making you happy or accepting you for you. You will finally receive someone made above all for you.
Learn to reap the rewards for your good deeds and your

good heart. You are worth it. Practice doing what's right and you will see great benefit.

The Rude of You

Everyone handles pain, sadness, guilt; and even joy and excitement in different manners. On occasion, when someone is emotional or feeling hurt, they can become irrational and say things that should not be taken personally, or; at least that is what you would hope. Imagine anytime emotional pain is involved: take death, break-ups or any other type of ill-prepared loss. For the sake of this blog; I'll take break-ups for five hundred, please, Alex!

      Many times it will not come as a surprise if your significant other acts like a fifth grader and says vindictive, undeniably rude, irrational or downright mean things to you. Supposedly, they do not really mean it. They are plain old hurt and desiring attention from you. I think it is what we would all agree as a moment of desperation! I don't think it even matters to them if they get a positive, negative or indifferent reaction, so long as they can conjure up something.

      Maybe you're a "Judgmental Judy" and think what I just wrote was the most absurd thing you have ever heard of. Perhaps you don't think it happens or you, and I do mean, just you, have not experienced it before. Let us then take death- which can be one of the most difficult times for many people of the world of all races, ethnicities, and backgrounds to handle.

      It is a time when old war wounds and intense emotions can take and sometimes break down families and pull them apart. No matter the root of resentment or contempt it can often times cause dissension, friction and skeletons to fall from places you never could have imagined.

Still looking at "Judy" in the mirror eh? Then let us take the loss of a job or any other loss of a major source of income. Think of the recession America has been going through. Sometimes, out of sheer frustration, a person will say something irrational and plain rude to someone else in an effort to get their point across. Even in the ding dang on Starbucks line someone could be rude. If you still cannot relate, just go crawl back under the rock you came from. You are a rare exception.

I do not know how many of you have been the observer or offender, but I do know, I was taught, or possibly learned it along the way of this thing called life that after some trial and error, of course, I have to be careful of what I let depart from my mouth. I learned through the Word that there is power of life and death within the tongue and whatsoever a man speaketh so is he.

I supremely try and think before I speak. I've slipped on that more times than I'd care to bring up but, I will say; I do usually mean exactly what I say, and hardly ever; if not have never went back on what I say. I have been both blessed and cursed with the gift of gab. I am blunt. Unapologetically straightforward and I say what I mean and I mean what I say.

Yes, yes, yes I know sometimes we all have said things in the heat of an argument that you may have felt, later on, was below the belt, however; it takes practice not to renege on statements that fly from your mouth too often. I am just saying; it saves you on all that apologizing in the long run. Keep in mind apologies begin to lose value if done too often.

Music

Isn't it amazing how music, a single song, can place you right back to the setting you were in when you first heard the song? Not only the setting, but that exact moment, emotion and even sometimes conversation you had. Music is so powerful. It brings moments back. It takes you right there. It does not matter if it was a good memory, great memory, bad memory, or sad memory just hearing the music or the words from that song places you in that moment all over again.

Advice to Service Providers

How are you a nail tech and underneath your fingernails are dirty? How do you style hair, and your hair is raggedy? How you are in fashion, own a boutique, and are not yourself fashionable? How do you advocate and sell health and wellness when you, yourself, are not healthy or well?

Take a page from Corporate America, Small Business Owners and contract workers. When you work for companies you are required to wear and sell their brand, right? Why wouldn't you use that same, exact, initiative when you work for yourself? Who better to advertise and brand your ideas, your gifts, and your talents than yourself?

Cosmetologists, artists of makeup, stylist of hair, and any of the others that are not mentioned; you attend classes and schools to get licensed, correct? If we wanted to look like clowns after makeup applications, if we wanted to burn our faces and necks with hot irons, if we wanted to misalign our eyebrows or scold ourselves with hot wax, if we wanted to leave from the salon looking worse than we did when we arrived, if we wanted to nip our toes or cuticles with burning electric files or razor sharp utensils we could stay at home, keep our money, and do it all ourselves

However, we do not desire to do that. We come to you all with a specified craft because you are the professionals so we expect professional work. With that being said, we return to the mantra; if you don't look good, you won't feel good. Please provide your customers with the particular quality service they require.

Lumps on Logs

When you are factoring your decision to respond to an event invitation please consider: If you can't skate, don't attend a SKATE party. If you're not going to dress up, don't attend the COSTUME party. If you're not into games, don't attend a GAME night. If you don't like to read, don't join a BOOK club. If you don't indulge in meat, don't attend a BARBEQUE. What do you think will be served? It certainly will not be only fruit trays and salad.

The moral of the story: Participation is the purpose for your extended invitation. If you will not participate in the required or, shall I say, specified activity, do everyone a favor and regretfully decline. You serve no good purpose watching everyone else partake in the said activities. You tend to make others feel uncomfortable ogling and on looking instead of taking a part in the fun. Seat holders are only useful at award shows, and even then; they ask you to clap, cheer, and stand at particular times.

All I am saying is that it is bothersome to the other guests and especially the host if and when you don't participate after saying you would by accepting the invitation. Acceptance of the invitation usually signifies that you have an understanding of theme, time, place, and activities. It is a sure-fire way to never be invited again. After all, that is the point of extending an invitation, you know? The request that you will participate or at least, what is that word: ATTEMPT.

End of Your Rope

Have you ever found yourself at the end of your rope? You are at your wits end. You feel as if you are about to lose your mind. Question is: who hasn't? Who has not been there in that place hanging on to the end of the rope?

At that time and in that moment go head and go into that private area. It is your special place that no one knows about except you. Sob, cry, yell, scream, get pitiful if you need to, cry some more, and then; get up, get over it, and MOVE. Give yourself the permission to go through that private process. No one needs to know or has to know. You will find your strength in that place. It is your private intervention. You will find your peace. Within that storm, you will find the calm.

Some People...

There are some people that never, seldom ever, see the good in things. To some people the glass is always, almost empty and there is probably no more left anywhere for a refill. These type people could ruin a wet dream, as the expression goes. Just know that what some mean for bad, God will make your good.

I've seen some instances of this theory as I am quite sure, many of us have. We know that all things work for the good of those that love Christ and sometimes, even those that are "working on it" and aren't quite there in their faith get some residual effects of those around them that do believe whole-heartedly. Count it all joy.

Look for the positives in your situation. Be an active spectator for those positives. Trust me, it is not always easy but, do not start creating negatives in your situation. Creating issues can be easy to do when you are feeling down and not so positive. Life already kicks us around enough try not to do this. Hush all that negativity in your mind and silence the mental adversities you might conjure up. Weight will eventually get lifted.

Don't Get Mad, Get Even

If and when someone says you are not cut out for something, or that you are not good enough for something or someone. Prove them wrong, don't get mad, and in fact give a big smile. It confuses your enemies. Yes, they are enemies, because if someone is not for you then they are against you. Now friends, if they don't know about it; they are not against you. Maybe they don't agree with you, or perhaps they are not on the fighting lines with you. In this case, they are not your enemy.

They still support you. They still want the best for you. Maybe you just forget to mention something to them. Do not run around thinking everyone is an enemy. Instead of getting mad at the real people that attempt to steal, kill or destroy your dreams and positive thoughts. You own your dreams. No one can deny the power thereof or take them from you. Be a fighter for what you want or believe in because if you don't believe in yourself; you cannot expect anyone else to do it.

Word to the Wise

Please be careful in life with those that you call your friend; those that you associate with, those you confide in, those who you enjoy a good time with. Honest and true friends are rare. A friend that you can count and depend on is a definite life gem. There are also so many magnitudes of friendship. Many people believe in the saying keep your friends close, and your enemies even closer. Well I don't need an enemy close to me. In fact, remove them please and thank you.

I say be careful and tread lightly with folks you call a friend because there are some people in the world that are miserable. Hopefully, they were not in any way born in actual misery, and hopefully they were not born miserable. Here is to the assumption that they have may have gotten miserable with age and time. It could be due to life circumstances or poor choices on their part, but whatever their excuse; they turn out to be miserable.

Misery loves company. In their misery, they will pretend to be your friend by laughing at your jokes, extending a shoulder for you to cry on, offering sound advice, and wishing you well in all of your endeavors. All the while they are the same "friend" that hopes you fail, gives the advice they actually followed to get them into their miserable predicament, laugh when you cry, and gives a side eye to your funny jokes instead of genuinely laughing.

Does any of that sound familiar? Maybe not, your "friend" is probably well disguised or revealed as the frienemy.

The frienemies are just that. There's no special formula to them. They are the enemy that pretends to be your friend. Often times, especially in getting to know you, they sincerely attempt to befriend you. It may have started off well, then a change occurs, and they become envious of you for whatever reason neither of us will ever recognize.

They envy your life. They desperately just want to be around you, know you, understand you, and your life. The problem is; the frienemy is misguided and does not know how to be a true friend. Instead of support, they challenge everything you stand for. Some of them do not just challenge; they actually work double time to disprove, discredit, and flat out slander you. Some people thrive on an amiable competitive edge; however, the frienemy does not actually challenge to uplift you what so ever. Their main concern or goal is to crush you under their heel. If it sounds harsh, that would be because it is.

I ask again; why is keeping enemies closer than friends important or a way some of us live? Enemies are not in your life for anything other than trouble. Leave them where they are. Send them back where they came from. They are not wanted. Having that enemy or hater should just drive you further along in your goals if you move further away from them. The difference between a hater and an enemy is their approach.

At least the enemy is bold enough to reveal themselves and make it known, meanwhile; you probably have someone in your life right now that's been a hater since pre-kindergarten. That just means we should be careful with our inner circle. We don't have to dismiss friends. We are just cognizant of the people we trust with our life. Aspire to be surrounded with positive, uplifting, good and whole-some people!

Standing

To be standing in the same spot, doing the same thing, never, in reality, ever achieving anything is a curse. It has to be some type of curse to also be chasing your tail, like a dog would. The problem is changing the current situation from standing still. The solution to that problem will be what makes us conquerors, mighty warriors in the world we live in, or cowards, victims of what lies ahead. Which do you choose? How do you choose? You only get one life and it is important to make everything count for you, not against you.

M.O.V.E.

Don't allow being in a rut to define or dictate your lifestyle. Sometimes when we lose a job, a family member, status in life, etcetera it can and will cause you to get into a rut. I like to call it a funk. Sometimes your mindset can cause this funk. It does not always have to be an intentional loss; sometimes we have our own private battles within our minds, bodies and spirits. I'm here today to say M.O.V.E. past it.

Motivate yourself out of your funk. Concentrate on the good and positive in your life.
Organize your thoughts. Contain your thoughts. When you feel negativity creeping in; dismiss those thoughts, feelings or desires. Force yourself to think happy thoughts. Recite a scripture, say a prayer, or read an inspiring message. Make it your business to focus on the "happy" of life regardless the circumstances surrounding you or that you are standing in the center of.

Value yourself. Come to the decision that you matter to someone, somewhere. No matter how point-less, worth-less, or inefficient you may feel; understand that your purpose is far greater than anything you could or will imagine. Know there is more to life than what we are seeing.

Emerge yourself in positive changes. Hustle-up onto a quantity of good fortune. Create your own opportunities of happiness. Then, and only then, will you begin to see the rainbow through your storms. No one is beyond cloudy days, thunderstorms, and natural disasters, however; it's all about recovery.

Single Girl Gems Part Deux

SGG 15 If you make mud pies you're going to get dirty.
*Stay away from the so-called rude boys, bad boys, or any of the other silly endearing terminologies we have provided them. Just like the old saying; you can't turn a whore into a housewife. It remains the same for these types. They could be fun but that is all.

SGG 16 Become Dora the Explorer
*Have an exciting date with your city. Go with girlfriends or alone. Tested, tried and true; it is better to go alone.

SGG 17 Letting go of past relationships is not saying I hate you; it is saying I love me.
*Ladies, leave the EXtosterone alone. There is a reason why you are no longer with them. Get out of the way of your next relationship.

SGG 18 Being alone is perfectly ok, as long as you are not lonely. If you are feeling lonely, re-read this book.

SGG 19 Do not block your blessings.
*Try to be a nice, inviting person. It is not you against the world of men. Do not openly male-bash. Do not take personal frustrations, which nine times out of ten; we cause ourselves, and use them as a conversation piece. Please, please, please do not, for the love of all things Louis Vuitton, air your dirty laundry.

SGG 20 Wait on the ring.
*Do not go around wearing a fake, or real, diamond on your left ring finger. The Mr. Right that saw you across the room and took an interest just saw you wave with that left hand, so he kept on walking.

SGG 21 Be an asset and not a liability.

SGG 22 Learn something.

*Be a better you and not for anyone, but yourself. This will ensure you have something positive to offer to any relationship.

SGG 23 Every now and then a girl should splurge on herself. Reward yourself for hard work and good behavior.

SGG 24 No matter the circumstance practice being thankful for where you are and what you have in life. Remember perfect practice makes perfect.

SGG 25 Go for it.

*Whatever "it" may be, go after it. Do the impossible and be enthusiastic about making it happen.

SGG 26 Take caution with those that whisper I love you in one ear and shout I hate you in the other.

SGG 27 Everyone is not like you, all you can do is pray and move on.

"Change your attitude, change your life!"
~Khrystian Nichole

Khrystian Nichole was born and raised in Texas, where everything is bigger. She is a Prairie View A&M University graduate with a degree in Communications (Radio/Television) and a minor in Dance.

Currently a highly qualified 5th grade science teacher in Dickinson ISD, a musical theater director/choreographer for Theater Under the Stars, Creative Director for her dance company, Crowd Pleasers Entertainment, and pursuing her Master's degree in Educational Administration. Khrystian Nichole is often times a writer of blogs, juvenile fiction, poetry, adult fiction, Christian fiction, self-help, and non-fiction. Among those things, she is an avid reader, coloring book diva, karaoke Queen, love enthusiast, and water walker. When asked what motivates Khrystian to continually seek success she says, "Every story has an ending, but in life; every ending is just a beginning! I'm not afraid to pursue my dreams especially when it seems impossible; life is too short not to LIVE!"

Connect with her at www.khrystiannichole.com

www.ingramcontent.com/pod-product-compliance
Lightning Source LLC
Chambersburg PA
CBHW060516100426
42743CB00009B/1339